A PICTORIAL HISTORY OF
SCIENCE FICTION FILMS

A PICTORIAL HISTORY OF
SCIENCE FICTION FILMS

DAVID SHIPMAN

HAMLYN

To Van Phillips
– *in the hope that this will convert him*

Endpapers: *The living quarters on Io. Recreations pursued by the mineworkers in* Outland *take some dubious forms – but someone is providing for them.*

Half-title: *A scene from* Star Wars.

Title page: *The Disney studio has been adept at fantasy since the first artists did the first drawings for its founder, Walt, in the 1920s. Apart from 20,000* Leagues Under the Sea *its sci-fi movies tended towards the cute, but when it returned to the genre it did so with great seriousness – and lavish spending, as you may guess from this superb design for the spaceship which has been stuck in the* Black Hole *which gives the film its name.*
© Walt Disney
Productions 1984

Right: *The city of the future, from* Things to Come.

CONTENTS

Published 1985 by
Hamlyn Publishing,
a division of The Hamlyn Publishing Group Limited,
Bridge House, London Road,
Twickenham, Middlesex.

ISBN 0 600 38520 5
Printed in Spain

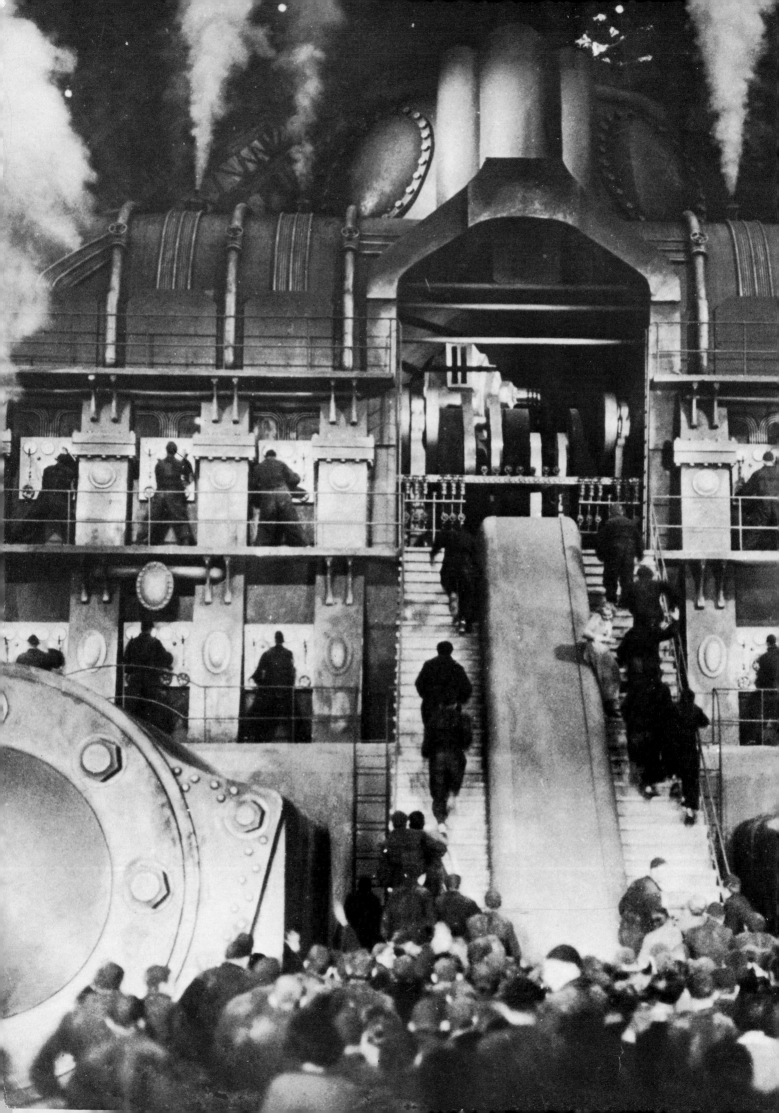

CHAPTER 1
Magic Realized

In Metropolis, the city of the future, the workers live deep underground, toiling endlessly at the huge machines. But even the most oppressed workers will revolt. A scene from Fritz Lang's Metropolis.

THE oldest surviving literatures that we know are of a fantastic nature. So, to come much nearer our own time, are the Greek myths, and many of the tales collected in the Bible. Man's quest for knowledge of the moon and the stars – of other planets, of the past, of the future, of faster ways to travel, of the ability to fly like birds, travel to the ocean-bed, of life after death, of undiscovered places, was more likely to be of a speculative than a practical nature; and thus many imaginative writers set down their thoughts for the wonder of others. During the Renaissance, Leonardo da Vinci tried with charts and drawings to work towards some findings about some of these matters. But despite those who, in the succeeding centuries, made discoveries about the universe and the human body, it remained a field for the romancers and necromancers. In 1785 Rudolf Raspe published, in English, his account of the adventures of the German soldier and explorer, Baron Karl Friedrich Hieronymus von Munchausen (1720–97), embroidering them, to the baron's delight, so that he appeared as a superman of the time.

Europe was at the threshold of the Romantic era. The 18th century trend towards classicism had been countered by a vogue for the Gothic, as exemplified by Horace Walpole's 'horror' novel, *The Castle of Otranto*, published in 1765. A flood of Gothic novels followed, but the Romantic era brought something new, a novel which might be said to have shown the way to modern science fiction. In Mary Shelley's *Frankenstein, or The Modern Prometheus*, published in 1818, Dr Frankenstein creates a form of human being in the laboratory – a being who grieves because he has no soul. Further experiments in another laboratory cause a Dr Jekyll to find that he has two souls – or, at least, having transformed himself into Mr Hyde he becomes a very different sort of person. This doctor and his *alter ego* was the invention of Robert Louis Stevenson, who published *The Strange Case of Dr Jekyll and Mr Hyde* in 1886. He was not the only writer to remain interested in the strange and macabre in that materialistic age, but he was the only one writing in English whose fancies were of a scientific nature.

In France, Jules Verne published *Five Weeks in a Balloon* in 1863 and *Twenty Thousand Leagues Under the Sea* in 1870. His only true heir is H. G. Wells, whose *The Time Machine* was published in 1895, the very year the Lumière brothers opened the first cinema, in Paris. It is hardly surprising that the cinema and science-fiction should arrive together. If we look to Verne, as we should, as the founder of true science-fiction, we can find in his work a manifestation of the urge to invent and discover on the part of his contemporaries. Few of the new-fangled devices happened overnight – not, anyway, as far as the man in the street was concerned. In the second half of the 19th century, in the ever-expanding cities, a small number of people were having their houses lit by electricity instead of gas, were getting used to the gramophone and the telephone. Many people were travelling to work in an underground railway in London, Paris and New York but were not aware that horse-drawn vehicles were doomed by the development of the internal combustion engine.

It was an age of wonders; only three years into the new century the first heavier-than-air machine would take flight at Kitty Hawk.

Like many of man's new marvels the cinema was not invented; it evolved. Three elements were involved: the film, the screen and the projector. By the 1880s several scientists and experimenters had found methods of photographing consecutive images which could be viewed in machines that turned – of which the best-known was Edison's Kinetoscope. It was not a satisfactory method, especially as the magic lantern had projected images on to screens for over two centuries. By the 1890s several inventors had patented projectors into which could be threaded the celluloid roll film devised by George Eastman in 1888. By 1895 the privileged in several countries had seen moving images projected, but it was in December of that year that the public saw them too, for the first time, on payment of an entrance fee. That was in Paris, courtesy of two scientists, the Lumière brothers. Within two years motion pictures – which could best be described then as animated views – had become a feature of music-hall bills in most major cities. The subsequent developments, like the origins of movies, are outside the scope of this book – and anyway, by that time the cinema had already discovered its capacity for fantasy.

Since the showing of motion pictures seemed fantastic enough to the first audiences its capacity for what we might at this stage call 'magic' surprised no one. The man who discovered that, and by accident, was Georges Méliès (1861–1938), a professional illusionist. His fascination with spectacle began as a child with a puppet theatre and in 1888 he abandoned his father's footwear factory to run the Théâtre Robert–Houdin, where he had appeared as an amateur. He was tremendously excited by the Lumières' first films but they refused to co-operate with him, so in 1896 he purchased Edison's Kinetoscope films and from abroad also – Britain – his projector. Films became a feature of the magic shows at the Théâtre Robert–Houdin, and with a camera of his own devising and film stock also bought from Britain he began to supplement his material with shots taken in the streets of Paris. One day, projecting his film in the laboratory, he saw a carriage transformed into a hearse. In fact, the camera had jammed. Other practitioners had realized that the film could be stopped in the camera and restarted with a different view, which was what Méliès did now. Within days of his malfunctioning camera his theatre patrons were watching *L'Escomptage d'une Dame* (1896): a woman sits on a chair; she disappears; a skeleton is discovered on the seat, to disappear in turn and be replaced by the woman. In *Le Magicien* (1898) the magician, played by Méliès himself, constantly vanishes and reappears in various guises on different parts of the stage, as well as turning himself into inanimate objects.

Méliès turned out dozens of such films, as did his competitors, copying him wholesale. In *L'Auberge Ensorcelée* (1897) a man (Méliès) in a hotel room is subjected to a moving candle, an exploding candle, a collapsing chair, shoes that walk away and vanishing clothes. Such items were in

Mary Shelley and Robert Louis Stevenson both invented men of inquiring mind, Dr Frankenstein and Dr Jekyll respectively. Dr Frankenstein constructed a robot in the image of man, while Dr Jekyll, well before the age of Freud, started to research the darker side of his nature. Both stories would be turned into successful films in the early 30s, discussed in the next chapter.
Left: *Dr Frankenstein (Colin Clive) discusses his creation with Dr Waldmann (Edward Van Sloan) watched by his assistant, the hunchbacked Fritz (Dwight Frye).*
Below: *Dr Lannion (Holmes Herbert), gun in hand, watches Dr Jekyll (Frederic March), transforming himself back from Mr Hyde. The experiment has overwhelmed him and he spends more time as his evil alter ego than as himself.*

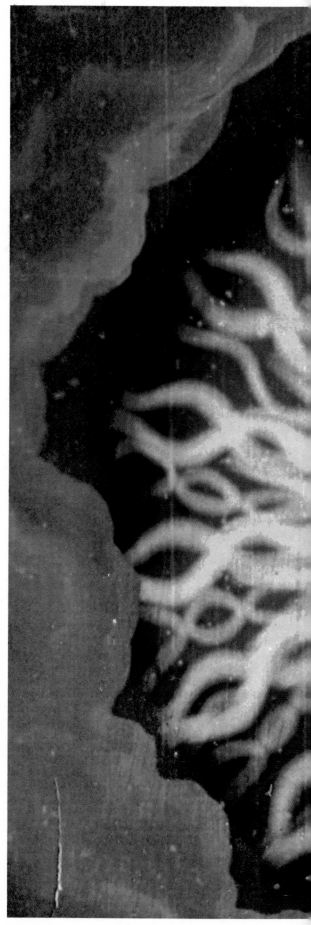

Méliès' sense of fun made the Man in the Moon a character in several of his films: a rocket ship arriving on the moon was, literally, one in the eye of that lunar gentleman. The gag was repeated in several films, so here is the sun in Voyage à Travers l'impossible, *getting tired and thinking of bedtime.*

accord with the policy of Méliès's theatre, but he also regarded it as the home of spectacle. Since it could not compete with the grander and greater Paris theatres he began to film reconstructions of actual events and well-known stories. The latter tended to be versions of fairy-tales, and Méliès favoured Oriental stories so that fakirs and genies could indulge in the tricks for which they are noted. He also liked ghost stories; but if there was any profession more congenial to his work than that of magician it was that of scientist. In their laboratories scientists could indulge in weird experiments and the one in *L'Homme à la Tète de Caoutchouc* (1902) has fashioned a real head, which lies on a table – and by applying bellows to it he can make it large or small, which in cinema terms meant that Méliès had discovered an advancing or retreating camera as well as superimposition.

In common with his contemporaries, Méliès did not understand narrative – nor did he ever seem to understand it as developed by others. He was instrumental in the move towards longer films, but his most ambitious was hardly more than the animated series of tableaux that he had turned out to that time. This was *Voyage dans la Lune* (1902), in which he plays a professor trying to interest a company of savants – in the hats and cloaks of wizards – in a trip to the moon. The meeting ends in chaos but a rocket is constructed and launched – after being pushed into the mouth of a cannon by some scantily-clad girls. Like a miracle it disappears, and is found stuck in the moon's eye. It is a movie of invention and good humour, but its success the world over amazed Méliès.

Of all the planets the moon, for obvious reasons, has most fascinated mankind. The end of the 18th century had seen some notable discoveries about the solar system, adding greatly to the speculations which had continued since ancient times. A further discovery was made in 1846 (of the existence of Uranus) and in 1865 Jules Verne published *From the Earth to the Moon*. Wells's *First Men on the Moon* was issued in 1901 and if Méliès was not responding to the further findings made about the solar system in the interim the two books helped to create a climate acceptable to film. Cinemagoers, then, were hardly sophisticated or indeed educated, given that the medium was much despised for frivolity; but the original audiences of *Voyage dans la Lune* would not have found it entirely beyond the bounds of probability. Méliès himself acknowledged his debt to Verne – and we should note that he had already issued a short comedy, *Mésaventures d'un Aéronaute* a year earlier, perhaps in response to *La Conquête de l'Air* made by his rival Ferdinand Zecca for Pathé. Zecca's trick films were often the equal of those of Méliès, and from the evidence we have those of Gaston Velle, supervised by Zecca, often surpassed them. Looking at the filmographies of the three men (many of the films have disintegrated) we find similar titles throughout. For Pathé Velle made *Voyage autour d'une Etoile* and later, in Italy, *Voyage dans une Etoile*, but certainly it was Méliès alone who became renowned for these films. He hoped to improve on his greatest success in making *Voyage à travers l'Impossible* (1904), which is twice as long – indeed, it may have been the first two-reel movie, and at the time was reckoned

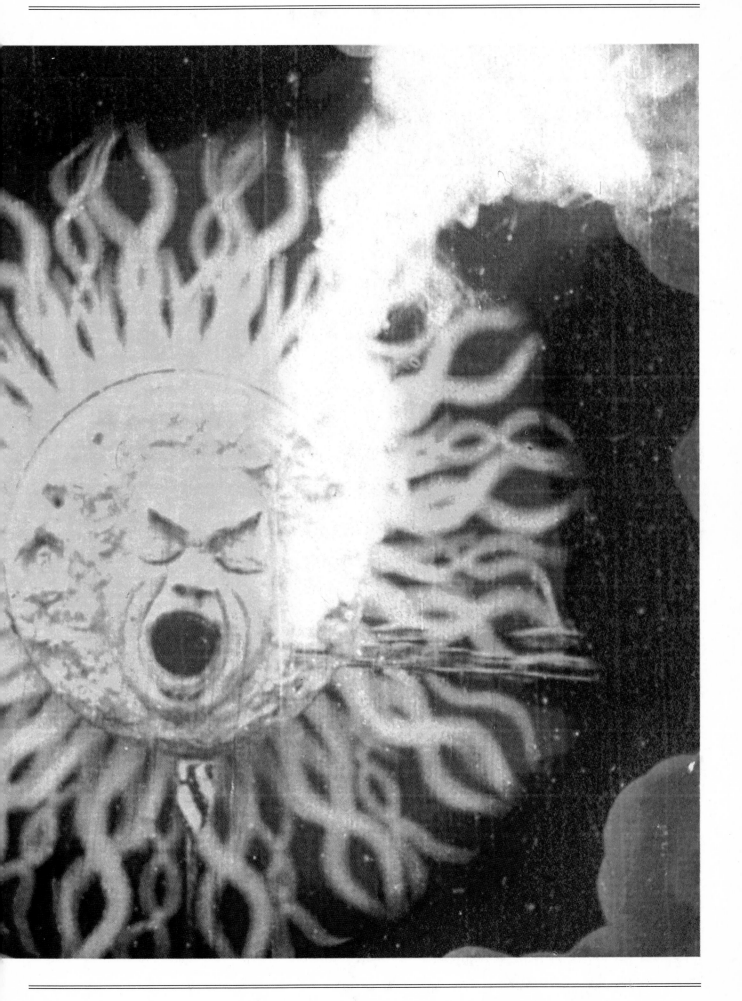

Right: *The wise men preparing the launching of the rocket to the moon in* Le Voyage dans la Lune, *one of the seminal magic films directed by Georges Méliès, who saw to it that the occasion was decorated with pretty girls - clearly the forerunners of the cheerleaders who accompanied the triumphant astronauts of a later age.*

Below: *Fantasy went out of fashion in movies with the decline of Méliès, but it particularly attracted René Clair. In* Le Voyage Imaginaire *the young hero (Jean Borlin) seeks escape in dreams from the teasing of his colleagues, but somehow they have got into the dream as well – Jim Gerald, left, and Albert Préjean, right.*

to be the most expensive yet made. The action is not dissimilar to that of *Voyage dans la Lune*: a professor announces a new machine to take another group of savants on an unlikely journey. The contraption turns out to be a railway train capable of climbing mountains or travelling under the sea. Between the two it takes off for the sun, to repeat the chief joke of the earlier film (the machine in the eye of the moon/sun, a man's face made up); again there is a broad sense of irreverence, but the piece is a little hard to appreciate today. People pile in at a painted railway station to travel on a painted train through a painted mountain-range – though there is a real waterfall, and such details are endearing.

The new medium, the cinema, was evolving rapidly, but Méliès was unable to adapt to the changes. In the years that followed he made films whose titles tell us that he continued in this particular genre: *Le Dirigeable Fantastique* (1905), *La Magie à travers les Ages* (1906), *Vingt Mille Lieues sous les Mers* (1907), *Le Tunnel sous la Manche* (1907), *La Photographie électrique a distance* (1907), *Le Raid Paris–New York en Automobile* (1908) and *A la Conquête du Pole* (1912). Many more of the early films have survived because they were more popular and many more copies were circulating. Few of the later ones that I have seen show much advance on the early ones: *Le Fakir de Singapour* (1908), though pleasing enough in itself, does raise the question as to whether audiences were not by this time utterly tired of trick films. The promisingly-titled *Hallucinations du Baron de Munchhausen* (1911) is certainly amusing, with a Muppetlike dragon (which is transformed into a spider woman), but the baron's dreams are resolutely earthbound. By this time Méliès was in debt to Pathé, which had become his distributor, and he made his last film in 1913. Two years later he converted his studio in Montreuil into a theatre and returned to illusionism on stage. In 1923 he was declared bankrupt but a belated recognition of his work began in 1928, when he was discovered selling toys in Montparnasse.

Among those delighted as a child by the Méliès films was the great director René Clair (1898–1981), though he came to the cinema as theorist and intellectual. Nevertheless the first film he directed is a fantasy, *Paris Qui Dort* (1924) – and, indeed, it was retitled *The Crazy Ray* in Britain and the US. As a film critic, Clair believed that the cinema should return to the aesthetics of the time of Méliès, that the camera existed to record movement. So, in a Paris which is motionless, a group of people dart from one *quartier* to another. A night watchman on the Eiffel Tower descends to find the Parisians are under a spell – or most of them. He finds a small group of people who have escaped, so to preserve them he takes them back to his lofty perch, where they themselves go almost numb from boredom. That is broken by a sudden radio call, telling them to go to a certain house in a certain street, where a girl informs them that her scientist father is putting the world to sleep with his magic ray.

This *jeu d'esprit* made Clair's reputation and, following his theories, he made another comedy – and his first feature, *Le Fantôme du Moulin Rouge* (1925). Despite the title, it is not really about a ghost, but its theme depends on the cinema's ability to provide superimposition. A businessman visits the Moulin Rouge, where his melancholy expression attracts the attention of a doctor. Shortly afterwards the man disappears, but a reporter (Albert Préjean) on his trail finds his body in the house of the doctor, who claims that all he did was to separate the man's body from his spirit – which is now mischievously creating havoc throughout Paris. The police are about to perform an autopsy when the spirit learns that his beloved adores him after all; and the latter part of the film is of his chase to unite himself with the body in time to prevent the surgeon making the incision. Clair designed *Voyage Imaginaire* (1925) as a tribute to Méliès. It is about magic, though in the form of a dream – one that occurs to a timid bank clerk (Jean Borlin) who is being razzed by two colleagues. It is a three-part dream – or journey – taking in fairyland, the top of the cathedral of Notre Dame and the Musée Grevin, where the waxworks come to life most convincingly, with stiff movements and painted eyes – the best part of this quite short piece. Clair clearly thought that screen humour consisted in invisibility, objects moving of their own volition and similar tricks till he changed direction with *Un Chapeau de Paille d'Italie* and the success of that was such that he thereafter used a more human, more gentle, type of comedy. But many of his later films were based on outlandish or fantastic conceits.

Un Chapeau de Paille d'Italie, though based on a 19th century play, is basically a 'chase' comedy – and it was the profusion of chase comedies which had made Méliès seem old fashioned. Those chase comedies developed with the help of star comic players and the melodramas that followed hard upon them introduced to movies the heroes and villains of the dime novel. With them came the serial, ending with hero or heroine in such dread predicament that audiences could be relied upon to return the following week to see whether and how they extricated themselves. Among the most famous of these are those made in France by Louis Feuillade, *Fantomas* (1913–14), *Les Vampires* (1915) and *Judex* (1916–7). The first and last of these are named for their villains, who were influenced by the popularity of Arsène Lupin, the gentleman master-thief created by Maurice LeBlanc. Since Lupin's speciality was disguise, both Fantomas and Judex went further in this respect, able to transform themselves – most notably into human flies – and to appear and disappear magically, making it tough on their upright pursuers. Since both men wanted to be as powerful as possible they may be considered forerunners of that constant villain of the genre, the man bent on world domination. The other staple villain, the mad doctor, probably appeared first in France, in *La Folie du Docteur Tube* (1915), directed by Abel Gance. The doctor in this case, with an enlarged cranium, experiments with animals and humans, changing their size. This experimental film is a comedy, intended by its maker to demonstrate the camera's ability to distort perspective.

Gance at that time considered himself an avant-garde film-maker, as did Clair at first. In France it was intellectually respectable to show an admiration for the cinema, as it was emphatically not in Britain or the United States. In Germany, the cinema attracted writers and producers from the theatre, versed in catering to the public. In its early days the German cinema was seen as a medium for the fantastic and grotesque; if we study German literature or even the German character we should find reasons for that, but German film-makers seized the opportunities to show matters uncommonly suited to their medium. In 1913 the theme of Dr Jekyll and Mr Hyde turned up in *Der Andere* and in 1916 the idea of Frankenstein was converted into *Homunkulus der Führer*. Another version of that concept had already been seen in *Der Golem* in 1915, but it is with the first remake of that, in 1920, that the great age of the German grotesque cinema begins.

Its star, director and co-writer was Paul Wegener (1874–1948), a former actor with Max Reinhardt's company, who had made his screen debut in 1913 in *Der Student von Prag*, which he also helped to write – borrowing from a number of sources, since the student concerned sells his soul to the devil. Wegener played both rôles, for the concept was considerably more imaginative than that statement suggests. The *Student* makes a contract with the devil, who demands as his price the other's mirror image; and since the devil appears in the guise of a sorcerer he is able to conjure that image from the looking-glass. In time the student falls in love with a countess, whose fiancé challenges him to a duel. Since the student is an expert fencer it is considered an unfair competition, so he agrees not to harm his opponent. The devil, however, ensures that he is delayed in arriving at the appointed spot, and then, taking his place, kills the other – so that the student is disgraced for not honouring his word.

Wegener was a large man with a face that might have come from the steppes of Asia. This gave him a sinister, if not exotic appearance. Clearly, he found the role of the Golem congenial. He

In the 1920s the German film industry produced a remarkable series of films – notably those directed by Gerhard Lamprecht – which took a harsh and serious look at the dreadful condition of the country, suffering from defeat in war and inflation. However, the films which the Germans themselves preferred, and which they successfully exported, were the fantasies of a somewhat frightening nature.

Right: *Conrad Veidt in* Der Student von Prag *(1926), talking to his beloved, played by Eliza La Porta, while the devil (Werner Krauss) lurks nearby. Both films were remakes of others, now lost, made in 1913 and 1915 respectively. Paul Wegener, till then a stage actor, devised the first* Student von Prag *as a vehicle for himself, and he both produced and acted in the first* Der Golem.

played it in 1915, when he co-directed, and again in 1917 in a light-hearted sequel, *Der Golem und die Tanzerin*. According to Jewish legend, the Golem was created in medieval Prague by the Rabbi Ben Yehuda Loew to defend the ghetto against a pogrom. In the 1915 version he is an antique statue brought to life by the dealer, who places the Star of David on his chest. The Golem then proceeds to fall in love with his daughter, whom he jealously pursues when she goes to dance with her lover. The 1920 version, written and directed by Wegener and Henrik Galeen, restores the story to its traditional setting – and could thus be retitled *Der Golem: Wie Er in die Welt Kam*. The Rabbi Loew foresees disaster for his people and thus fashions from clay a robot, the Golem, first made by a magician of Thessaly who left an account of the secret in an ancient book. There is indeed trouble for the Jews. The Hapsburg emperor orders their expulsion, news of which is brought to the ghetto by the knight Florian, a handsome fop with a gap in his teeth and a rose in his hand. The rabbi brings the Golem to life by placing the appropriate magic word in the Star of David that he wears about his neck, and takes him to Court when he goes to plead for his people. The emperor recalls the rabbi as a magician, one capable of conjuring up visions from the history of his people – during which the roof starts to fall. The Golem holds it up, and in return the emperor revokes his edict against the Jews. But alas, back in the ghetto, Florian is

seducing the rabbi's daughter. So her sweetheart sets the Golem on to them, and he, after throwing Florian from the battlements, makes off with the young lady – thus fulfilling the warnings of the ancient treatise, that the Golem becomes dangerous when the heavens shift. The Golem runs amok till he meets a child, whom he takes in his arms; the girl playfully pulls off the star of David and the Golem falls to the ground lifeless.

This is, even today, an extraordinarily vivid film, and with its contemporary, *The Cabinet of Dr Caligari*, it ushered in a spate of German films of gloomy fantasy. They are usually referred to as the German Expressionist cinema, partly because the extravagantly painted sets of *Caligari* were clearly not realistic – and in view of its world wide success the German film industry poured out dozens of films with similar sets, of which the public tired so quickly that some were never released. However, *Caligari* is about madness; and just as Expressionist painting was often linked to darkness, either real or emotional, so are these films. *Caligari*, with its roots in the theatre, was a fluke; but at that time, after a serious defeat in war, there were deep-seated reasons why audiences did not want to watch dramas of everyday life. But if *Caligari* proved to be a dead end, there was mileage to be had from making audiences' collective flesh creep.

To return to the 1920 *Der Golem*, it is only just that it should borrow so heavily from *Frankenstein*, for the story of the Golem was recounted in *Fantas-*

Above left: *Paul Wegener in the title-role of* Der Golem *(1920).*

Above: *Conrad Veidt as Cesare the somnambulist in* The Cabinet of Dr Caligari. *Cesare was one of Caligari's fairground attractions in a small town plagued by a series of murders, leading the young hero in time to the unknown terrors of a lunatic asylum. The painted settings were a matter of expediency, but were widely copied because of the film's world-wide success. But the public soon tired of the gimmick and many of the later movies in this manner went unreleased.*

The moment in Nosferatu *when the crowing of the cock announces that dawn is officially here – and since the fearsome Count (Max Schrek) has lingered he meets his overdue end.*

magoriana, which we know the poet Shelley read to his wife and the guests staying with them in Switzerland in the summer of 1816. His guests were Lord Byron, who had already published *The Giaour*, touching on the nature of vampirism, and John Polidori, whose *The Vampyre* was published a year after Mary Shelley's novel. These were the sources which inspired Bram Stoker's novel, *Dracula*, which concerns a Transylvanian Count, apparently dead, who goes abroad after sunset to seek nourishment in human blood. Sinking his fangs into human throats, he sucks out so much that his victims are left apparently dead, too, and can only continue as vampires themselves. Following *Der Golem*, Henrik Galeen wrote *Nosferatu, eine Symphonie des Grauens* (1921), plagiarising Stoker's novel to such an extent that his widow was able to sue and have all prints of the film suppressed. In all cinema history these two prototypes – the themes of robot and vampire – have been so linked that it should be emphasized here that only the first really concerns us, despite the elements of fantasy in the second. *Nosferatu* at least introduced world audiences to the work of the director F. W. Murnau (1888–1931), whose *Faust* (1926) is one of the most stunning of all movie fantasies. This is of course the legend best known from Goethe's epic telling of it, of the old man who makes a pact with the devil in order to have his youth restored to him for the sake of a beautiful girl he covets. The magnificent opening of Murnau's film is a duologue between the aged Faust (Gosta Ekman) and Mephistopheles (Emil Jannings) on the good and evil that exists on the earth upon which they are looking down – and since this is a Silent film the argument has to be told in images.

At one point they take a magic carpet ride – and that is one of the several conceits taken from another fantasy by another master director, Fritz Lang, *Der Müde Tod* (1921). This is a four-part film, the sections linked by the first story, in itself based on a sentence in the Song of Solomon, that 'love is stronger than death'. A woman (Lil Dagover) loses her husband to Death (Bernhard Götzke), but he will be returned if she is able to prevent three deaths in time past.

Lang's ambitions took him to a thriller so long that it was issued as two separate films, *Dr Mabuse der Spieler*; and then, encouraged by its success, he tackled at similar length the *Nibelungenlied*, the Middle High German saga, probably dating from the 13th century. Some elements of the story were used by Wagner in his *Ring* tetralogy (the stories are quite different). Although Lang had the Wagner operatic scores arranged and adapted to accompany his two films, known together as *Die Nibelungen* (1924), he believed that only the cinema had the capacity to render the magical elements of the tale. The second film, *Kriemhelds Rache* is a straightforward tale of revenge and bloodshed, but *Siegfried* is witness to Lang's belief. Siegfried (Paul Richter) is, after all, a warrior from the north who must slay the giant dragon and overcome Alberich, the King of the dwarf Nibelungen, who has the power to become invisible during their contest. And Siegfried himself is able to assume that power, for he defeats the King, who rather unfortunately materializes while they fight, and robs him of the *tarnhelm*.

Lang's co-writer on his films till then had been his wife Thea von Harbou (who was to remain in Germany when he fled rather than take on the leadership of its film industry, as requested by the Nazis). She alone is the credited writer of *Metropolis* (1927), though he worked with her – and certainly conceived the idea, while on board ship in New York harbour and looking at the skyline

Murnau's version of Faust
is one of the most
imaginative of all Silent
films, but the pictures
which have come down to
us give little idea of its
beauty, which is most
notable in the Prologue
(left) where the aged Faust
lectures his students.
Below: *Faust (Gosta
Ekman), rejuvenated,
with Emil Jannings as
Mephistopheles.*

After Fritz Lang went to Hollywood he specialized in tales of contemporary life, usually involving murder, espionage and/or injustice. He made his name in his native Germany, however, with some fantasy films which were very ambitious for their time. Influenced by the great Swedish director, Victor Sjöstrom, Lang followed his example by turning to legend and came up with the two-part Die Nibelungen. *In the first part,* Siegfried, *Paul Richter plays the title-role and is seen here after the movie's high spot, his duel with the dragon. (Said beast creaks a little by the standards of today's movie monsters, but he remains impressive.) Siegfried, hoping to become invincible, bathes in the dragon's blood. But a linden leaf falls on his shoulder and a vulnerable spot remains.*

of Manhattan. He later denigrated the film, as did H. G. Wells at the time ('a soupy whirlpool'), but in science fiction – and this is the first true sci-fi movie – there were then no guide-lines. Almost certainly, however, Lang and von Harbou were influenced by *Wir*, a novel by the Russian writer, Yevgeny Zamatian. Following the Revolution in his own country he had envisaged the logical conclusion of a state run by a party machine instead of individuals – a society governed by science, reason and the need for utilitarianism, but one, in other words, in which we cannot feel optimistic. This is the Dystopia, as opposed to the Utopia created by Sir Thomas More. *R.U.R.* – the title stood for Rossum's Universal Robots – a remarkable drama by the Czech, Karel Čapek, written in 1921, had been successfully performed in most European capitals and the word robot had entered the languages of Europe. (*Robotnik* – forced labourer or serf). Not surprisingly, elements of that found their way into *Metropolis*, as well – to judge from the film itself – as details of the lives of the workers at the huge armaments factory in Essen, as regimented by its owners, the Krupp family. The hierarchy among the Krupps was also reflected in the film in the relationship between John Frederson (Alfred Abel), the boss of the city Metropolis, and his son Freder (Gustav Frölich). Since theirs is a struggle for souls, it is not unlike that which begins *Faust*.

This is the year 2000 AD and Metropolis functions smoothly, its zombie-like workers living far below the ground and being brought up to take up their toil, sheeplike, in shifts. Freder begins to question the inhumanity with which they are

treated, and when his father summarily sacks the loyal foreman for a minor error, he takes the side of the workers. The workers are in fact rumbling into protest, listening to Maria (Brigitte Helm). Freder had in fact stumbled on her while preaching – 'Between the brain that plans and the hands that build, there must be a mediator' she had said – and his admiring glances show that his decision to join his 'brothers' is not entirely altruistic. One day, while he searches for her, she goes missing, captured by a mad inventor (Rudolf Klein-Rogge) employed by the senior Frederson to make – as it turns out – a robot in her likeness. So the 'evil Maria', as the intertitle calls her, stirs up the workers to revolt in such a manner that they can be quickly quelled. But Frederson and the inventor find that they do not have the control they expected, so that the revolt gets out of hand, resulting in the destruction of Metropolis and the flooding of the subterranean dwellings. The workers' children are saved by the good Maria – miraculously rescued – and Freder; and because he thought his son lost, too, John Frederson sees the error of his ways.

It has been suggested – by the critic Frank Vreeland – that another source poached was *When the Sleeper Wakes* by Wells, and that the flooding of the underground city was borrowed from a forgotten novel about the end of Atlantis. *Metropolis* is such an eclectic work that we may suppose the repeated representations of the Seven Deadly Sins to be taken from *The Four Horsemen of the Apocalypse*, while the mob rioting at the climax would certainly have been influenced by *The Hunchback of Notre Dame*, if not the 1920 *Der Golem*. Crowds storming

Opposite: *Hollywood was quick to learn from European cinema. Fritz Lang introduced a magic carpet in* Der Müde Tod *(1921). Douglas Fairbanks had both a carpet and a flying horse in* The Thief of Bagdad *(1924).*

The vulgarity of much movie advertising belongs to a later era than the 20s, when audiences were acknowledged to be at their least sophisticated. Much of the art-work of the period might give later generations pause – and certainly Douglas Fairbanks was meticulous in such matters.

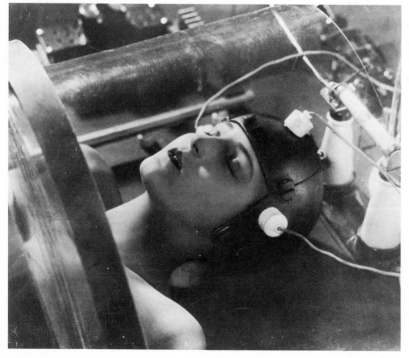

Lang's most famous fantasy remains Metropolis, *which may be the first true science-fiction movie as we now define the genre. Certainly it is set in the future, in a Dystopia where the outlook is grim for all but a handful of capitalists. Equally certainly much of it is mumbo jumbo, but it has a force so strong that it was not surprising to find it playing in commercial cinemas in 1984, with a new, specially composed score. These pictures give an excellent idea of its visual power.*

Opposite top: *Metropolis itself, showing the city of the privileged.*

Bottom: *The false Maria (Brigitte Helm), shown as a robot under construction.*

Left: *The true Maria, also Fraulein Helm, trying desperately to close the water gates and save the workers' children when the system breaks down after the workers' revolt.*

across the screen was a common feature of the Silent cinema, so was such symbolism as the use of the Seven Deadly Sins. At such points *Metropolis* has dated, though at the same time it remains visually impressive: the huge furnace which turns into Moloch in the hero's imagination; the electronic transformation of the robot into Maria; the Bible story, as told by Maria to the workers, with the scenes of the building of the Tower of Babel; the flooding of the city; the robot Maria dancing the shimmy before a host of white-tied admirers; and the climax, with the magician scrambling over the cathedral roof with Maria in his arms.

The achievement of *Metropolis* was so immense that it virtually brought to an end the fantastic period of the German Silent cinema – though Lang himself was to make *Die Frau im Mond* (1929). During this time some similar films were made in France, but due less perhaps to the needs of audiences than the personal predilections of those making movies. It was an age of full-blooded romanticism in literature, and the Belgian-born director Jacques Feyder filmed Pierre Benoit's popular novel, *L'Atlantide* (1919). The tradition that a whole continent lies under the Atlantic Ocean goes back to Plato, writing in 335 BC – though modern research suggests that the myth is founded on that volcanic eruption in modern-day Santorini (Thera) which destroyed the Minoan civilization in the Eastern Mediterranean. Benoit placed Atlantis somewhere in the Sahara, or at least it is reached by there – if you are unlucky enough, for the Queen's emissaries look for men to become her lovers. When she tires of them they are kept in coffins thereafter and displayed in the trophy room. The image of the woman as predator started in Italian movies before the First World War, but was given added impetus by the conflict, for women had been able to prove themselves

in jobs once considered the prerogative of men. Another all-powerful femme fatale was the centrepiece of *L'Inhumaine* (1924) directed by Marcel L'Herbier. L'Herbier was a great experimenter and innovator; in *L'Inhumaine* the chief attraction was the decor, which was to form and influence Art Deco. The story is even sillier than that of Feyder's film, but it does have an element of fantasy. Georgette LeBlanc, who commissioned the film and provided some of the financing, plays a famous singer worshipped by a number of men: an American industrialist, an Indian maharajah, a Russian-born revolutionary poet and a French engineer. She entertains them at parties which feature Oriental dancing and they are waited upon by servants in masks and knee-breeches as they vye for her favours. The engineer fakes suicide after she has refused his hand, but materializes when she goes to identify the body in his laboratory. There she is enchanted by seeing her fans around the world on television (so-called, incidentally, in the intertitles) but her carryings-on have caused her other suitors to realize that she prefers the engineer to them. Of the dastardly tricks to which she is now subjected, the worst is the poisonous snake deposited in a bouquet by the maharajah. She is hurried to the laboratory with no hope of living, but the engineer gets every light and piece of machinery there working, so that she does survive, via science rather than medicine. The film was not a success; indeed, according to the French film historian Georges Sadoul, its 'errors and extravagances marked the end of the impressionist movement'.

The British were rather prosaic about such matters, even if a love interest was introduced into *The First Men in the Moon*, which Gaumont produced in 1919. This was the first of Wells's novels to be officially filmed, though as early as

One reason for the revolt in Aelita; the suppressed Martian workers, forced to wear these helmets so that the rulers can monitor their thoughts.

story is a melodramatic rigmarole, and what follows is a great simplification. Presumably on the supposition that audiences would not accept life on Mars, several parts of the film are supposed to be a dream, while the leading actor Nikolai Tsereteli plays two roles, that of Spiridonov, who designs a space-ship, and Los, the hero, who later disguises himself as Spiridonov. Los has a frivolous wife whose friends long for pre-Revolutionary days; disgusted, he dreams of life on Mars, and from Mars Aelita (Ioulia Sointseva) looks down and falls in love with him. Awake, Los helps to build the new Russia; asleep again, he dreams of two friends, Goussev (Nikolai Batalov), a Red Army soldier, and Kravtsov (Igor Ilinski), a comic detective. The latter is on the trail of Los, so Los impersonates Spiridonov, but the detective is also after Spiridonov, who is supposed to have murdered Los's wife. There is a confrontation between the two, with Goussev present, in the space-craft, which promptly blasts off. They arrive on Mars, which has enough mayhem of its own, with Aelita's maid under arrest for having murdered Aelita's lover. Aelita wants Los, hoping that she will help him lead a Revolution as overwhelming and magnificent as that of October 1917 – but clever Los knows that she is a false revolutionary, planning to become a dictator. As he murders her, he imagines that she is his wife, at which point he wakes up. The narrative then returns to the very beginning of the tale, to be followed by a ten-minute mix-up of chronology, dream and reality intermingling, and a sequence to atone for some heavy-going elsewhere.

Contemporary admiration was centered on the Martian settings, designed by Alexandra Exter and Isaac Rabinovich of the Moscow Kamerny Theatre, at that time noted for experimental work. Today these are not of great account and the film's chief interest is as the work of two major figures of Russian cinema, the director Yakov Protazanov and Fedor Ozep, who adapted Tolstoi's original novel.

Neither was to do anything similar in films, and the other Russian science-fiction film of the time was such a failure that it led to the disbandment of the collective which had produced it. That collective was led by Lev Kuleshov, the credited director, and the writer was Vsevolod Pudovkin, later a celebrated director – and he plays a supporting role in the film concerned, *The Death Ray* (1925). The aims of the collective were to make the sort of movies with which Hollywood had captured world audiences, without ideology if necessary. What the collective failed to appreciate was that audiences were accustomed to Hollywood's narrative clarity – and that is something singularly lacking in *The Death Ray*. It is not even clear whether it is set in Paris, pre-revolutionary Russia or an unnamed European country. The workers, anyway, have risen against their bosses, who have called in fascist forces to bring down the ringleaders; so the workers, apart of course from their solidarity, have only one hope – the death-ray, the invention of a kindly scientist (Sergei Komarov). It takes a while before it can be effective, and we are meanwhile in the world of the old serials, with such devices as poisoned cigarettes and stolen plans.

1895 he gone into partnership with Robert W. Paul, who was excited by Wells's novel *The Time Machine* and believed that it could be adapted for the new medium. Paul had developed a motion picture projector and in October 1895 he and Wells patented the concept of audiences being taken on simulated voyages in time and space. Their ambitions received a setback when, later that year, the movies 'arrived', but Wells did not lose his enthusiasm for the new medium. In 1914 he signed a contract for the production of some films based on his novels, but war intervened; *The First Men in the Moon* cooled his ardour. It was not a success, and was to have no successors in Britain for more than a decade.

Among those influenced by Wells was the novelist Alexei Tolstoi, though from the film of his novel, *Aelita* (1924), we may suppose Zamatian's *Wir* equally influential, though the authorities had not allowed it to be published in the Soviet Union. *Aelita*, conversely, finds much to admire about the changes in Russia, though set for the most part on Mars. Like *Metropolis*, the

The American cinema, meanwhile, remained disinterested in the possibility of space travel or the machinery of the future. The 'science-fiction' films then made, less than a handful, would not have been considered outlandish by American audiences. The old bogeyman, Hyde, appeared in a new version of Stevenson's story, *Dr Jekyll and Mr Hyde* (1920), directed by John S. Robertson primarily as a vehicle for the virtuosity of John Barrymore, one of the most admired actors of the day. Barrymore's Dr Jekyll is underplayed and he is Hyde for most of the time, scampering about like an animal, demonic of eye but otherwise slave to his make-up – which remains startling. The film's foreword asserts that we all have good and evil within us, and 'all our lives the fight goes on between them and one of them must conquer'.

This is, of course, a study of the macabre, but with a very Victorian view of the world in which alcohol and sex are as close to evil as murder and physical maltreatment. To our eyes today there seems nothing wrong for a doctor to go from surgery to a music-hall; and since many of us enjoy sexual and alcoholic indulgence there seems no reason why we should be transformed into a monster to do so. Still, when in a music-hall a girl (Nita Naldi) shows a yen for Dr Jekyll he, in the words of the intertitle, 'for the first time in his life had wakened to his baser nature'. After discussing with chums the possibility of man having two

separate bodies for his two beings he has concocted that potion which transforms him from a handsome man to a decrepit old monster. It is not entirely clear why that girl agrees to live with this creature but, anyway, 'as Hyde plunged deeper into vice, his trail was littered with victims of his depravity'. We do not, however, see them, except for the girl. Nevertheless, the piece remains effective.

It cannot be said that this film was influenced by European models – indeed, a dramatized version had been successful in New York a few years earlier – but we may suppose that *The Magician* was so inspired, though based on an early novel by Somerset Maugham which M-G-M purchased in a job-lot with *The Moon and Sixpence* (which they never got round to filming). The director was Rex Ingram, one of the most prestigious of those under contract, but it was made in Nice, along with others of Ingram's pictures, for there was no love lost between Ingram and Louis B. Mayer, the head of the studio. The magician of Maugham's novel was modelled after Alisteir Crowley, but the story is not unlike *Frankenstein*. The magician's lair in this film is so much like the laboratory in the most famous (1931) version of *Frankenstein* as to suggest that it was studied by the later film's art director. Paul Wegener journeyed from Germany to the Côte d'Azur to play the title-role, a man fascinated by the mysteries

Readers of Somerset Maugham would hardly guess that this still represents a scene from a movie version of one of his novels. A scene from The Magician, *which was much more lurid than the novel. This dream sequence shows Alice Terry in the clutches of a spirit supposedly conjured up by the magician himself. (Compare the picture on page 79, a later example of Hollywood conjuring up a Greek satyr to represent tempting evil.)*

of life and death. He has discovered an antique formula to create man scientifically, but it needs the blood of a young maiden – and thus eventually the magician, Haddo, spirits away our heroine (Alice Terry). She falls under his evil influence, so that her uncle and fiancé remove her to a clinic. Haddo recovers her, and is about to perform the operation – in the midst of the obligatory storm – when her nearest and dearest return to fight for her. The fantasy sequence is much influenced by two earlier films, the Danish *Witchcraft Through the Ages* and the American *Dante's Inferno*, made by Fox in 1924.

Fox also made *The Last Man on Earth* (1924), one of the most freakish movies of the period – indeed, of any period. It is set in the future, in 1940, presumably on the assumption that audiences would otherwise not accept a society in which all males over the age of fourteen have been carried off by an incurable disease – except one, Elmer (Earle Foxe), who has survived in a remote part of California, where he is discovered by Greenwich Gertie when her plane crashes among the redwoods. She and her gang capture Elmer and put him up for auction – and the excitement causes the Stock Exchange to re-open after ten years. The custody of Elmer is debated in the Senate: one senatoress thinks that he should be turned over to her, to start an 'intellectual' race, but it is eventually decided that the two prettiest senatoresses should stage a boxing-match, with the winner getting Elmer into the bargain. Apart from the foolishness – the costumes are particularly bizarre – this movie has a nasty air, not least in a quasi-pornographic sequence when some young ladies in a clinic ply Elmer with drink in order to have

their way with him (but he collapses, dead drunk). Perhaps the intention was a burlesque, a variation on the famous revue sketch, 'If Men Played Cards as Women Do', but it is amusing only unintentionally. It does make one wonder about the mentality of all involved, including the director, John G. Blystone.

A more orthodox example of the genre is *The Lost World* (1925), directed by Harry O. Hoyt and made by First National at the behest of Willis O'Brien (1886–1962), whose interest in stop-motion cinematography had earlier resulted in a one-minute movie about a monster on the top of an office block in San Francisco. As a result of that a local producer-exhibitor commissioned him to make *The Dinosaur and the Missing Link*. There followed *The Ghost of Slumber Mountain*, with the requisite models made by a young Mexican, Marcel Delgado. But that a major studio was now interested in O'Brien's work was due to the addition to his team of Ralph Hammeras, who had recently developed and patented the system of glass shots. The screenplay of *The Lost World* is based on Conan Doyle's novel and starts in London where Professor Challoner (Wallace Beery) is lecturing on dinosaurs, which he maintains still exist on an unexplored plateau in the Amazon. A colleague has disappeared there, though fortuitously leaving a diary. The dead man's daughter (Bessie Love) accompanies Challoner on an expedition, together with a cub reporter (Lloyd Hughes) and a baronet (Lewis Stone). They find prehistoric animals all right, though these are unimpressive today. However, the final sequence remains powerful: instead of Doyle's climax, a battle between the heroes and

Another rather endearing monster from the Silent era, in this case a dinosaur threatening Bessie Love in The Lost World. *Either this one or one of his fellows will be taken to London, where he will escape and cause havoc. That wasn't in Conan Doyle's book, but the situation would recur in what is perhaps the most famous movie fantasy of them all.*

ape men in the crater of a volcano, the film's makers have substituted a dinosaur in London – having been captured and shipped home – on the rampage. He falls off Tower Bridge and is last seen swimming out to sea, but apart from that the finale resembles that of O'Brien's finest achievement, *King Kong* (1933).

In Germany the *neue sachlichkeit* movement had caused the expressionist films to die out; the best German films of the second half of the decade are realistic studies of low life and prostitution. Consequently there is a different tone to the three other major fantasies made in Germany in this period, though in *Alraune* (1928) Paul Wegener

was again up to no good, as reunited with his old colleague, Henrik Galeen, who directed. This is the second and most famous of the six films based on Hans-Heinz Ewer's novel, published in 1911. Alraune is an artificially-created woman and one therefore without a soul. Ewer's inspiration may have been, yet again, *Frankenstein*, and/or a now forgotten French novel, *L'Ève Future*, by De L'Isle-Adam and published in 1887, about an inventor who creates a beautiful automaton, who is christened Hadaly and believed to be a real woman. So is Alraune – according to the 1928 version (there had been an earlier one, made in Hungary in 1918 by Michael Curtiz, as its director was

'Go, and catch a falling star, Get with child a mandrake root' wrote John Donne, the most famous reference in our literature to the medieval belief that the mandrake plant was half-human. Something similar was the genesis of Alraune (Brigitte Helm) in the film of that name, and that was why she was so destructive. (There have been at least four film versions.) She is seen her with Alexander Saschia.

renamed on arriving in Hollywood). Her name corresponds to our mandrake or mandragora, that root in the shape of a human body found beneath a gallows. Alraune's father is said to have been hanged and her mother to have been a prostitute, but in fact she is the creation of a professor (Wegener).

The British film censor baulked at the idea of scientifically created life, so the intertitles ignored this, to concentrate on the hereditary influence in explaining our heroine's destructiveness. From the start Alraune (Brigitte Helm) is what is usually referred to as 'a handful'. She persuades a young man to help her run away from school, but after they are working in a circus she is flagrantly unfaithful with the lion tamer encountered en route. Detectives recover her and return her to her 'father', the professor. But when, in the South of France, he refuses her hand to a vicomte (John Loder) and makes her read the journal of her life, we can hardly blame her for behaving worse than ever after discovering her origins. Nor, come to that, can we suppose her wrong to seek revenge on her creator.

In referring to *Am Rande der Welt* (1927) as a fantasy, I only do so because it is set in the future; it is otherwise a grim warning against the evils of war, as directed by Karl Grune, best known for *Die Strasse*. As the title implies, we are at the edge of the world, in border country: to the mill situated there comes a stranger (Imre Rady) seeking work. He is also a foreigner, soon in telephone contact with his own country and therefore instrumental in starting the War. War is declared as the villagers celebrate the 300th anniversary of the mill, to the vociferous joy of the young and the dismay of the battle-scarred older people. The mill is eventually captured by the enemy, and the miller's daughter (Brigitte Helm) is loved by two amongst them. One is the stranger who came to the mill, now about to betray his country for her, and a young officer (Jean Bradin), whose love she returns. The message is clear: that love is stronger than any loyalty to country.

Along with *Metropolis*, *Die Frau im Mond* (1929) is the only film of this period which may be said to be prophetic, and it was also directed by Fritz Lang and written by Thea von Harbou. It starts very well with a scientist informing a group of sceptical savants that there is gold on the moon. As an old man, he is sought for a trip to that planet by Professor Helius (Willy Fritsch), who is being financed by an international company. Once the explorers – a later generation would call them astronauts – get aboard the space-craft the action is uninteresting till, on the moon, it becomes laughable. The travellers include a boy stowaway and the inevitable woman, in love with the professor. The lovers must be parted at the end, for someone has to remain behind in order for the space-craft to attempt the return journey. The professor, as leader, decides that it must be himself, so he drugs the drinks of the others – only to find that the girl is waiting at base camp, not drugged after all. Some of the details are surprisingly naïf, too, such as the opening of the windows of the space-craft on landing; but Lang clearly went to enormous trouble to get the details as correct as possible. We may note that his two technical advisers went on to become leading figures in the development of rockets, Hermann Oberth in Germany, Willy Ley for the Americans.

Left: *It could not be said that Fritz Lang's movie about space travel,* Die Frau im Mond, *is an advance, either imaginatively or cinematically, on* Metropolis. *It does not have the same grandeur or amplitude, but there are moments when we can feel that primitive era (i.e. in space-age terms) shaking hands with our own.*

Far left: Am Rande der Welt *is one of the many memorable German films of the 20s, not least because of its powerful décor. If you arrived late, you might not think it science fiction, but it is in fact set in the future – a future which has not eliminated wars, a depressing refrain for people who had hardly recovered from the First World War. The young man being threatened is played by Imre Rady.*

CHAPTER 2
The Frontiers of Thought

The citizens of Everytown, a hundred years in the future, gathering to hear Theotocopulos, the master sculptor, who heads the movement against the coming flight around the moon. A scene from the second part of Things to Come.

IF, then, the last science fiction movie of the Silent era – *Die Frau im Mond* – is about interplanetary space travel, so is the first of the Talkie period. Curiously, air travel, though still at that time far from an everyday experience, had not been a feature of the very few futuristic movies that had been made. The movie companies were much more interested in airships – zeppelins. Cecil B. DeMille's *Madam Satan* (1930) which lies outside the scope of this book, had a party sequence aboard an airship which can only have reflected wishful thinking. However, the continuing expansion of air travel may have stimulated those who devised *Just Imagine* (1930), since in its opening sequence the hero (John Garrick) leaps from his own personal plane to lounge on the one being piloted by his girl (Maureen O'Sullivan). They are hovering above a vast city of the future – in fact New York in 1980 – and below them the air lanes of taxi-cabs and other traffic are being marshalled by stop lights and aerial patrolmen. The concept of this movie owes much to Lang's two films, even if it is *sui generis* – has there been a science-fiction musical since? The songs, which are poor by the standards of this particular team, are by Brown, De Sylva and Henderson, who indeed dreamed up the entire film; they penned the story and dialogue and served as Associate Producers.

Their idea of the future is a constant of the genre: as in *THX 1138* (1969) names have been replaced by numbers and sex is banned by the authorities. Babies are delivered from sidewalk automats, as is food – in pill form. Such things had not happened by 1980, and perhaps we are not supposed to take them seriously. But as a comedy *Just Imagine* is pretty painful, unless one admires the comic lead, El Brendel. He plays a man brought back to life after being struck by lightning fifty years earlier. He goes to live with the hero who, forbidden to marry his sweetheart by officials, accepts a commission to be the first man on Mars. Brendel stows away on the spacecraft, while Frank Albertson, the hero's friend, makes the third member of the expedition. Mars turns out to be pretty spikey, as to both apparel and architecture – and also deceptive, for the population is divided into two tribes, one wholly good and one completely evil, with matters complicated by their being identical as far as their rulers and their minions are concerned. Without knowing their language, the earthlings have a confusing time, but they do eventually escape from the wicked tribe, fighting its members off as they start up the space-ship for the return to earth.

The interior of the craft and the details of the flight are laughable today, while other aspects of the future are unimpressive. New York in 1980 has a form of phone-a-vision; a doorbell ring is signalled by a light and a noise emanating from a table, in which the arriving party can be seen. The clothes are unimaginative except for a dress that can be turned inside out for another occasion. The film is quaint, as in the song 'There's Something About an Old-Fashioned Girl' – that something being that they are jazz babies, cocktail flappers or whatever. But that New York setting is magnificent. It was the creation of Ralph Hammeras, credited with the special affects, and co-art director with Stephen Gooson. Ernest Palmer was the photographer and between them they have created a gleaming city of skyscrapers, some 250 storeys high, with as many as nine lanes of air traffic. The cost, huge in those days, was a quarter of a million dollars – such was Fox's faith in the project. The public refused to endorse it, a fact recalled for years to come in Hollywood production conferences whenever anyone suggested a story of the future.

That Hollywood did embark on a series of fantastic movies is due to that figure that we cannot keep from these pages, Count Dracula. A dramatized version of Bram Stoker's novel had been a success on Broadway in 1927 with Bela Lugosi, a Hungarian-born actor who usually played supporting roles in films. The grotesque element of the tale suggested to the management at Universal that it might be suitable for Lon Chaney, who had starred in its two biggest successes of the Silent period, *The Hunchback of Notre Dame* and *The Phantom of the Opera*. It had always been galling to Universal executives that they had let Chaney slip through their fingers, for he had gone on to be an even bigger attraction for M-G-M, chiefly in a series of horror films directed by Tod Browning, whom they had also had under contract at one time. Negotiations were in an advanced stage when Chaney died and had to be replaced by Lugosi, who was still playing the bloodthirsty Transylvanian count on tour. Browning had returned to Universal for *Dracula*, which the veteran Frenchman, Robert Florey, had been at one time set to direct, and it was he who suggested *Frankenstein* (1931) as a follow-up. Carl Laemmle, in charge of production, declined once more to put Florey in charge and he had no intention of borrowing Browning again when he had a contract director equally suitable – on the basis that he was English. This was James Whale (1896–1957), who had supervised the test of Boris Karloff (1887–1967), a supporting actor whose huge frame and melancholy appearance made him memorable in sinister roles. Lugosi had originally been scheduled to play Frankenstein's monster, but Universal didn't like the test he had made. Apparently Lugosi disliked the script – but in fact he hoped to coerce the studio into producing a new version of *The Hunchback of Notre Dame* with himself as Quasimodo.

The screenplay of this *Frankenstein* utilized not only Mary Shelley's novel but a dramatized version by Peggy Webling, produced in New York in 19??. Miss Webling had decided that in creating the monster, Frankenstein had accidentally used the mind of a criminal. This suited Universal's purpose in hoping to attract the audiences which had loved *Dracula*, so in the film the science student Frankenstein (Colin Clive) creates a being from bits of stolen corpses. Frankenstein's obsession cuts him off from family and fiancée, and like many of the obsessed he cannot contain his creation. From the ancients to the present there had been dozens of cautionary tales about those who tamper with nature. From the start the monster is dangerous and ungovernable. He murders Frankenstein's hunch-backed servant – ungratefully, since it is he who had provided him with that stolen criminal brain. It is only when the

Left: *Futureworld, or, anyway, Future-Manhattan, as envisaged and superbly realised by the designers at Fox (forerunner of 20th-Century Fox) for* Just Imagine, *a not very good film but one which, nevertheless, can justifiably be described as unique.*

Below: *El Brendel is resurrected after being dead for fifty years, another scene from* Just Imagine.

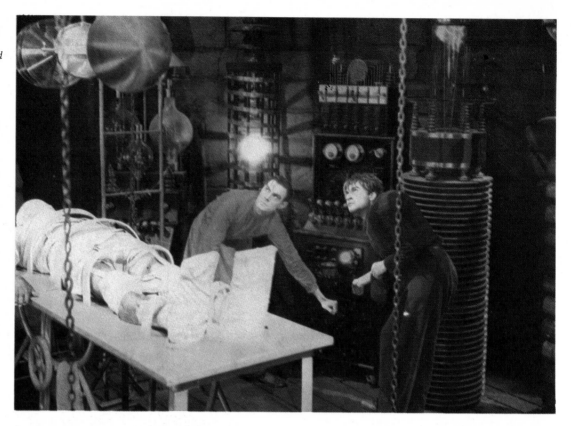

creature frightens his bride-to-be that Frankenstein comes to his senses. He decides that the creature must be destroyed, and the local population joins him in hunting it down. Karloff's interpretation – and the patented make-up – is the prime reason for this film's enduring popularity, but Charles D. Hall's art direction is wonderfully imaginative. Whale's work is also very skilful, never lingering over effects or taking needless chances. This is the definitive version of this tale, however far from Mary Shelley: it is not easy to forget Frankenstein's gothic, roomy laboratory, with its crackling electronics apparatus or the creature, with his inhuman groans and splayed walk.

The popularity of the vampire and the monster might have been partly due to the Depression. Audiences wanted escapism but had turned their backs firmly on the stories of vice among the aristocrats so popular a few years earlier. Gangsters, showgirls, reporters and shop assistants had taken over. America's favourite star was a middle-aged actress of ample girth, Marie Dressler, whose most familiar role – she played it at least three times – was as a make-do-and-mend wharfside worker. No case may be made for Count Dracula, with his gleaming white tie and tails, but audiences may have felt sympathies for Karloff's monster. Certainly all the Hollywood studios weighed in with tales of horror and/or the grotesque, many of them featuring Karloff or Lugosi.

Universal proposed a version of H. G. Wells's *The Invisible Man* (1933) to Karloff, but he was in the midst of a salary dispute with the studio, who accordingly offered the role to Claude Rains, a New York stage actor who, like Karloff, had a distinctive and British-accented voice. For that was all that the role required. Griffin, a scientist, has made himself invisible via a secret formula – one that unknown to him induces madness and megalomania. He dreams of ruling the world, and just for the hell of it creates havoc, including a train wreck which causes over a hundred casualties. He is caught when the police see him making footsteps in the snow, among several eerie moments. Others include his unwinding a bandage from his head, with nothing to be seen thereunder, and the pair of trousers (stolen from a policeman) walking down a street at night. Griffin becomes visible again as he dies in hospital, and if the doctor's attitude is somewhat sympathetic – Griffin is, after all, a mass-murderer – doubtless he has also been amused by the antics of a man who can make himself invisible.

Whale directed, and though he was to make only one more film in the genre it is the best of Universal's many sequels: *The Bride of Frankenstein* (1935), which is faithful to its predecessor, if not, yet again, to Mary Shelley. She appears in a prologue with Byron and her husband, but the main action, as in *Frankenstein*, is set in the present day. It turns out that neither Baron Frankenstein nor the creature were killed, after all. The latter has survived in an underground lake, and the baron is recovering from his ordeal when he is tempted by Dr Pretorious (Ernest Thesiger) into creating another artificial being. The original creature, again played by Karloff, is again on a murdering rampage. Pretorious finds him, befriends him and hides him away. He has him capture Frankenstein's fiancée in order to persuade the baron to cooperate with him – and they create a bride (Elsa Lanchester) for the monster, hoping thereby to tame him. Instead, she recoils in horror and rejects him, whereupon he begins to destroy everything in sight.

Universal continued to feature Dracula and

Frankenstein's monster in many sequels, made relatively cheaply and usually as supporting fare (to the main feature), despite the presence of such major actors as Rains and Basil Rathbone. Most of these films are outside the scope of this book, as are most of the other horror movies which emanated from Hollywood in the wake of *Dracula* and *Frankenstein*. Paramount made what are probably the two most impressive genre movies after those, to wit, a new *Dr Jekyll and Mr Hyde* (1932) and *The Island of Lost Souls* (1933). This version of the Stevenson story suggests that Jekyll's ventures into becoming Hyde are due neither to fidelity to science nor an enquiry into his sexual nature but simple frustration – for his fiancée's father forbids the wedding till it coincides with his own anniversary. Jekyll's transformations without the potion are much more frequent than in the other versions and if, understandably in context, he tries to murder his fiancée's father he also tries to murder her. The climax, when he is cornered by the police in his laboratory, is superbly handled by the director, Rouben Mamoulian, with Fredric March clambering all over it in simian manner. His performance, much admired at the time, seems to me to lack the weight and authority of Spencer Tracy in the 1941 version, and the famous transformation was more interestingly done in the later film.

The Island of Lost Souls is also based on the work of an important writer, in this case H. G. Wells, *The Island of Dr Moreau*; but with a lesser director than Mamoulian, Erle C. Kenton, it tends towards what a later generation would call 'camp'. Wells himself loathed the film – not unexpectedly, since Dr Moreau (Charles Laughton) is less a scientist-extraordinary than a mad one. Wells's theme, that self-knowledge can only be obtained by the destruction of innocence, is certainly lost. The plot is more or less intact, but Moreau's island is hardly established as a paradise which will be lost once it is discovered by those who are shipwrecked. These include Richard Arlen as the arch-hero, pitted against Laughton, an arch-villain – and very enjoyable he is too, smacking his lips as he says to Arlen, 'You're an amazingly unscientific young man.' The animals Moreau is turning into humans are less pathetic, as in the original, than grotesque – and they include Lugosi, in a minute role, as the 'Sayer of the Law'.

The British censor refused a certificate to this film, though not to the similar venture made by RKO, *The Most Dangerous Game* (1932), in which the shipwrecked guests (Joel McCrea, Fay Wray, Robert Armstrong) are sent out to the jungle to be hunted like animals by the mad Count Zaroff (Leslie Banks). This movie concerns us only because it utilized the same studio jungle, originally planted for *Bird of Paradise* (1932), as *King Kong* (1933) and because many of the same principals were involved. Co-director of the earlier film, with Irving Pichel, is Ernest B. Schoedsack, who directed *King Kong* with Merian C. Cooper, his co-producer on both films. Although *King Kong* is probably the most memorable of the horror and fantasy films produced in the US till that time – and perhaps to the present – its creators came to it not as purveyors of either fantasy or horror but as explorers and adventurers.

H. G. Wells's The Island
of Dr Moreau *became*
The Island of Lost Souls
*for picturegoers. On the
right, clearly, is a lost soul;
on the left is Dr Moreau,
played by Charles
Laughton with all the
bravura of which this actor
was capable.*

Merian C. Cooper (1893–1973) met Ernest B. Schoedsack (1893–1979) in Poland in 1920, while on a trip round the world. Both had served in Europe with the American army, Cooper as an officer with the Kosciusko Flying Squad and Schoedsack as a combat cameraman with the Signal Corps. Schoedsack had worked with the Hollywood producer Mack Sennett before the war, and inspired by the success of Robert Flaherty's documentary *Nanook of the North* they had persuaded Paramount to finance two similar projects, *Grass*, filmed in Iran, and *Chang*, which was shot in the jungle of Thailand. Also for Paramount they had collaborated on a version of A. E. W. Mason's novel *The Four Feathers*. While shooting that film in Africa, Cooper conceived the idea of a movie featuring gorillas, which he discussed with one of his colleagues, David O. Selznick. Selznick had made no decision when he moved across to RKO as head of production. RKO's finances were shaky and there was a danger of the studio closing. Selznick invited Cooper to inspect the books, and Cooper discovered one test reel and the script of a project called *Creation*, the brain child of Willis O'Brien, which was to utilize the processes he had used for the prehistoric animals in *The Lost World*. O'Brien abandoned *Creation* for a film about one – giant – gorilla. He and Cooper were encouraged by Selznick, but a test reel (it included the tree trunk sequence) was made before the studio executives gave the go-ahead. The screenplay was written by James Creelman (who had written *The Most Dangerous Game*) and Ruth Rose, apparently based on a story by Cooper and the best-selling thriller writer, Edgar Wallace (who died during production; in fact, his contribution was small).

Selznick later remarked that his contribution was to juggle the budgets of other projects, saving where possible in order to find the huge sum of $650,000 needed for *King Kong*. Apart from pre-production work, the actual filming took 55 weeks (most major films were then made in 4–6 weeks). The same systems were used as for *The Most Dangerous Game*: painted process foregrounds, some 'real' or studio jungle and then either painted backgrounds or back projections. Kong himself was only eighteen inches tall, though part of a real-size Kong was used for some sequences. The Fay Wray he plucks from the earth was an animated doll, though of course the real Fay, in close-up, was carried by a huge gorilla's paw. She was filmed first, and then her image projected frame by frame on a minute screen behind Kong, who was moved by animators between each individual shot.

If a few of the other monsters on Kong's island leave something to be desired the film is technically superb (even if an occasional seam may be spotted by the alert). The story itself is disarming. A film director, Carl Denham (Robert Armstrong), picks a starving girl from the streets of New York to be his leading lady in a movie to be made in the East Indies. 'You make movies in jungles and places?' asks Ann Darrow (Miss Wray). When they arrive at their destination, Skull Island, they find the natives living on the outer-side of a huge man-made barrier. In the darkness they kidnap

Opposite: *Kong himself, the king of all movie monsters. Here, in the 1933* King Kong, *he battles against a dinosaur on Skull Island, and (left) against the attacking planes on the top of the Empire State Building while Fay Wray lies swooning on the topmost ledge. Neither scene was repeated in the surprisingly successful 1976 remake. The later film's special effects creators did a magnificent job with Kong Mark II but perhaps felt that dinosaurs would be sub-Harryhausen, while Kong's climactic battle was transferred to the World Trade Center, which had replaced the Empire State Building as the world's highest structure.*

Ann from the ship and place her inside the gate of the stockade as a sacrifice to Kong. He snatches her up and kills several dinosaurs and such on the way to his lair. Setting off in pursuit is the crew, which includes Jack Driscoll (Bruce Cabot) who is in love with Ann. He rescues her. Denham is not a showman for nothing: he has been unable to shoot his film, but he has a monster to exhibit, if they can capture it. Kong's huge powers are overcome by gas. In New York he is bound by the strongest metal known to man and billed as 'The Eighth Wonder of the World'. What happens then must be known to most readers, but even so I am reluctant to set it down – though knowledge of this particular plot should not spoil the splendid entertainment provided.

Son of Kong (1933) begins with Denham, standing before a poster of Kong, being hounded by creditors – from whom he escapes by returning to the East Indies, with his friend Englehorn (Frank Reicher), who hopes to pick up cargo there. Englehorn's ship docks at Dakang, where they meet a showgirl, Hilda (Helen Mack), and the wicked Halstrom (John Marston) – who demands money from Denham, a hand-out from the proceeds of exhibiting Kong. He claims that it was he who had led Denham to Skull Island, towards which the ship is inexorably heading. Halstrom leads a mutiny, during which Denham, Hilda and the skipper are packed into a boat – to be joined on the island by the treacherous Halstrom, since the crew refuses to accept him as captain. Although the screenplay is credited to Ruth Rose, this section of it derives from *The Enchanted Island*, a 1927 film released by Tiffany, based on Shakespeare's *The Tempest*. What follows is not too much like *King Kong*, for the creature's son turns out to be a kindly, playful beast who has adventures with Hilda and Denham while a prehistoric monster keeps Halstrom, the skipper and a Chinese servant trapped in a cave. Hilda often refers to 'Poor little Kong,' and one may suppose that RKO were so delighted with the returns on the earlier picture that they decided to love Kong's son, literally, to death. The special effects are not derisory, as they have been claimed to be; the scenery – i.e. the matte work – is often taken from the original film, and the whole is professional and entertaining. This 'serio-comic Phantasy', as it proclaims itself, may have been rushed into production, but as it came out ten months after *King Kong* we may suppose the actual shooting to have taken almost as long as that.

Only Fox (if we except United Artists) remained uninterested in any but the most down-to-earth subjects – doubtless because of the failure of *Just Imagine*. At least, when the studio went travelling in time again, it was backwards, but bolstered by the box-office appeal of the great comic actor, Will Rogers and a script based on a story by the renowned humorist Mark Twain. *A Connecticut Yankee* (1931), directed by David Butler, features Rogers in the title-role, a radio repairman who, felled by a suit of armour in a big mansion one stormy night, wakes up to find himself at the court of King Arthur. He staves off execution by producing a cigarette-lighter. But this arouses the jealous wrath of Merlin, who demands that the execution proceed. Saved by a total eclipse of the sun listed in his diary, he soon has Camelot mechanised. 'I'll make 'em want things they didn't know existed and have been quite happy without.' In Twain's story the Connecticut yankee, a machine-shop superintendant, creates an industrial utopia in Arthur's Britain, based on American models, which he then destroys in a technological holocaust. In the film Rogers helps defeat the rebellious Morgan Le Fay (Myrna Loy) by organizing an army of automobiles and a gyroscope. Otherwise, Fox produced *Chandu the Magician* (1932), a fantasy based on a nightly radio serial and directed by Marcel Varnel and William Cameron Menzies, with photography by James Wong Howe. These three were among the leaders of their craft, though Varnel became best known for the comedies he later directed in Britain, and Cameron Menzies was chiefly famous for art direction (he was to be almost solely responsible for the 'look' of *Gone With the Wind*). At all events, they knew what they were doing, for *Chandu* is prime hokum, with no cliche overlooked and done with great elan and vigour. The trouble with Chandu is that although he can hypnotize, divide himself in two and is no slouch with a crystal ball, he is not always a match for the evil Roxor (Bela Lugosi), who has captured not only Chandu's brother-in-law but the death-ray invented by the latter. Possession of that will make him master of the world. The ray's electrical equipment is genuinely imaginative.

If Lugosi and Karloff were then among Universal's most notable assets, they were also in demand elsewhere; at M-G-M Karloff in turn was aiming for world domination in *The Mask of Fu Manchu* (1932), directed by Charles Brabin. Fu Manchu, the evil Chinaman dreamed up by the novelist Sax Rohmer, was always making such grandiose plans, if only to avenge himself on the white races. But although Paramount had featured him in some early Talkies this particular film is the only one usually regarded as science-fiction, perhaps because Fu Manchu's lair contains any number of live electric coils, ray-guns and other paraphernalia designed by Ken Strickfaden, who had invented the similar devices in Frankenstein's laboratory. The place is also replete with tarantulas, pools of starving alligators, spiked doors and half-naked black guards, only too eager to carry out their master's fiendish requirements. He and several British adventurers, including his customary adversary, Nayland Smith (Lewis Stone), are in competition to recover the sword and death-mask of Genghis Khan, believing that their owner can conquer the world. But the Britishers spend most of the time in Fu Manchu's clutches, where one of them, Terrance (Charles Starrett), attracts the libidinous attention of his daughter Fah Lo See (Myrna Loy). It is far-fetched, of course, and the dialogue is elementary, but the special effects are of a transcendental kind.

Tod Browning directed most of the similar M-G-M films of this period, of which only two concern us. Browning's *The Devil Doll* (1936) follows the exploits of two convicts who escape from Devil's Island. One (Lionel Barrymore), only wants revenge on the crooked bankers whose lying testimony sent him there; the other (Henry B. Walthall), wants only to perfect his experi-

Maybe, in the annals of penny dreadfuls, Sax Rohmer comes somewhere behind Bram Stoker and others: but Rohmer's Fu Manchu has had a long movie career, never appearing to more advantage than when Boris Karloff played the role in **The Mask of Fu Manchu**. *There is Boris, up to no good as usual in the centre of the picture; and there is Myrna Loy (later 'the screen's perfect wife') as his libidinous daughter hovering near her father's captive, Charles Starrett.*

It is hard to think of pukka-British Frank Lawton, left as a French taxi-driver, Toto. In a lobby card of 1936 (the film was not in colour) he beams at his beloved, Maureen O'Sullivan, under the apparently approving eye of her mother – sorry, father, played by Lionel Barrymore.

"Can I take you for a ride—in my taxi?"

THE **DEVIL DOLL** STARRING **LIONEL BARRYMORE**

A Metro-Goldwyn-Mayer PICTURE

A miniature Maureen O'Sullivan among the furniture. A publicity still from The Devil Doll.

ments, by which he can reduce creatures to two inches and then control their movements by projecting his own thoughts into their now otherwise useless brains. The two men combine their ambitions, with satisfying results to all except the unfortunate bankers – though perhaps it should be added they are not, in miniature, quite as impressive as those similarly afflicted in *The Bride of Frankenstein*. But the trick photography is not quite so outrageously clever. M-G-M also remade Robert Wiene's 1924 horror movie, *Orlacs Hande – The Hands of Orlac*, based on the novel by Maurice Renard, retitling it *Mad Love* (1935). The director was Karl Freund, who had photographed many famous films, including the 1920 *The Golem*, and who had directed a few, including (for Universal) *The Mummy*, in which Karloff, in the title-role, returns to life after 3700 years in his tomb. *Mad Love* introduces staples of the horror movie, a wax museum and a Grand Guignol theatre, before following the plot of Wiene's film – which it does with more conviction than the original. When Stephen Orlac (Colin Clive), a pianist, is injured in a rail accident his wife begs Dr Gogol (Peter Lorre) to help. Gogol, after 'assisting' at the guillotining of a murderer (Ed Brophy), who used to

have a knife-throwing act, grafts the latter's hands on to Orlac, whose father is stabbed to death after an argument with him. Later, again, the plot diverges from the original – as we may have supposed, since the Lorre role has been built up, and he is a remarkable villain. The film itself, though not made on a large budget, is a good example of what can be done when professionals use their skill at top measure.

Gabriel Over the White House (1933) is another matter – a considerable film in its own right, and one of the few films which tried to tackle the problems of the Depression in America. It starts with the inauguration of a new president (Walter Huston), who strikes us as affable and then ignorant. It turns out that he is completely without scruples or morals – and also irresponsible, so it is no surprise when he is killed in a car crash. Or, rather, he rallies, recovers – and in his new incarnation is the reverse of his previous self, now tackling the Depression, Prohibition and crime, as well as world peace, with farsightedness and skill. Eventually he begins to return to his pre-accident self, bowing to the party line, despite his secretary's claim that what he has done has made him one of the greatest man that ever lived. And she, when he has a stroke, withholds from him his medicine, so that he dies as a renowned and revered statesman, unable to undo the good that he had done. That, at least was the original ending – and the one used in Europe. But the film's implied criticism of Republican policies infuriated Louis B. Mayer and other M-G-M executives. The film's producer and director, respectively Walter Wanger and Gregory La Cava, soon left the company, and the film was only released because the newspaper tycoon William Randolph Hearst had encouraged Wanger to make it. Hearst's investment in certain productions released by the company, as well as his papers' endorsement of M-G-M films, was too important to lose (in fact, Hearst's newspapers had recently turned against the Republican party). However, a new ending was shot for American audiences, in which it is merely hinted that the President reverts to his old self as he dies. Many critics accused the film of preachiness, but it was one of the few political films of this era to appeal to the public.

If the Depression, as I've said, left Hollywood in no mood to produce more escapist fantasies, the German film industry felt differently. But that was probably because Germany's own troubles, caused by inflation, were being surmounted as the American Depression worsened. With the coming of sound, German audiences succumbed to movie musicals – both about ordinary people who sang as they went about their everyday chores, and the more traditional operetta-type, derived from the stage, of handsome hussars and crinolined ladies in marzipan settings. The producer of some of the most famous of these (*Die Drei von der Tankstelle, Der Kongress Tanzt*) was Erich Pommer, who had earlier been responsible for some of the greatest German successes in fantasy and science-fiction, including *Caligari*, *Faust* and *Metropolis*. The coming of sound had robbed Germany of its pre-eminent commercial position among the European film industries, but it was attempting to retrieve it by filming the same

Frances Drake and Peter Lorre in Mad Love, retitled for most foreign territories The Hands of Orlac, under which title the story is usually known. This was Lorre's first Hollywood film. World-famous since making Fritz Lang's thriller M, he is said to have turned down offers from the US to play similar roles. However, this one was freakish enough.

Down deep beneath the sea, in a vast laboratory, a greedy Scottish industrialist has constructed an atomic reactor able to turn lead into gold. He has kidnapped Hans Albers, at the bottom of the steps, in order to do so, but in this scene from Gold *Herr Albers is allowing his qualms to get the upper hand.*

story in German, French and English (so was the French film industry and, to a less aggressive extent, the British). Pommer was too astute a producer to copy Hollywood in attracting world audiences; remembering *Metropolis*, he planned a movie set sometime in the future, with spectacular scenes which could be used in three different language versions, with a different nucleus of leading players for the more intimate scenes. *F.P.1 Antwortet Nicht* (1932) centres on a plan to position a landing stage – the F.P. or *flugplatform* of the title – halfway across the Atlantic. The designer is Droste (Paul Hartmann) whose boyhood friend, Ellison (Hans Albers), now a famous aviator, steals the plan – for unclear reasons, except that they are in love with the same woman, Claire (Sybille Schmitz). Years later, the platform is functioning, with Droste in charge; Ellison has returned, penniless, from a long absence, and Claire knows that he is the only man prepared to fly her out there when F.P.1 does not answer – which, we know, is likely, since Droste's second in command is planning to sabotage it.

The English-language version starred Conrad Veidt in the Albers role, played by Charles Boyer in the French one. All three versions were directed by Karl Hartl, who made *Gold* (1934) also for Ufa – but without Pommer, who had had to flee Germany when the Nazis came to power. The star is again Hans Albers, playing Werner Holk, a scientist and colleague of Professor Achenbach, who has invented a machine for turning lead into gold by means of an atomic reactor. The machine explodes during an experiment, killing the professor, and Holk is offered a position by a Scottish industrialist, John Wills. Aboard Wills's

yacht, and also at his Scottish *schloss*, Holk is exposed to numerous mysteries. He also learns that Wills was responsible for the sabotage of Achenbach's machine. By a combination of threat, blackmail and coercion, he is obliged to work on a larger, more complex version in Wills's underwater laboratory. Lead is turned into gold, which becomes so plentiful that it touches off a world crisis. Holk decides to put a stop to this by destroying the reactor, which allows Albers his usual movie task of haranguing the crowd, forcing them to see the right and defy the tyrant. Indeed, despite the undeniable ambitions of this film it too often proclaims itself a compendium of German movie cliches – Wills becomes the usual last reel power-crazy maniac, deserted as usual by all and sundry and clinging to his machine as Holk pulls the controls so that the whole thing explodes and the sea pours in. The last sequence is impressive, with the electric charges flashing like lightning as we await the inevitable. The film was examined by the Allies at the end of the war, in the vain hope of finding some clues as to what the Germans may have known about nuclear power; and this particular final sequence was incorporated into an American B movie, *The Magnetic Monster*, starring Richard Carlson and written and directed in 1953 by Curt Siodmak – who had provided the original story of *F.P.1 Antwortet Nicht* and who as an exile provided the adaptation of the English version of *Der Tunnel*.

Der Tunnel (1933) was based on Bernhard Kellerman's Utopian novel, originally published in 1914 but given new topicality by the success of *F.P.1 Antwortet Nicht* – for this is a tunnel being burrowed under the Atlantic, from the US to

The entrance to The Tunnel, *with Leslie Banks looking down at some colleagues, including Richard Dix (in the white boiler suit), the driving force behind the tunnel. The lady at the bottom of the steps is Madge Evans, Dix's wife in the film.*

The Tunnel, in the film of that name. It went under the Atlantic – or at least was being constructed during the course of the story, as can be seen from the picture.

Spain. Its architect and mastermind is MacAllan (Paul Hartmann), whose backers include Mr Lloyd, who has invested $25 million, and Mr Woolf (Gustav Gründgens), with $10 million at stake – seemingly, though in fact much more, for he has acquired huge shares in shipping and as a consequence blackmails one of his henchman to sabotage the tunnel. There are also a number of sub-plots as directed by Kurt (later Curtis) Bernhardt, who was permitted by the Nazis to return from Paris to make the film at the behest of the French co-producers (the French language version starred Jean Gabin).

This flurry of science-fiction stories was to have no successors with the Nazis in control of the German film industry. In Britain, Michael Balcon, like Pommer, was seeking the sort of subjects which could be sold the world over and his interest in remaking *Der Tunnel* was in making a statement on Anglo-American unity. In fact, although *The Tunnel* (1935) also begins in the world of high finance, the plots of the two films begin to diverge after the opening sequences. The hero's name is similar, McAllan (Richard Dix) and he also wants to construct a tunnel under the ocean – and should be allowed to, as one interested party points out, since he had built the Channel Tunnel in 1940. In this version the wicked tycoon (Henry Oscar) starts to sell his shares in the project in order to create a panic, so that he can buy all others available at the lowest possible price. As in the original, McAllen is a fanatic dedicated to his work, and there are numerous floodings, cave-ins and other emergencies to be handled. But it also transpires that they are tunnelling through a subterranean volcano – and when it erupts into

the tunnel, McAllen orders the doors closed on the workers so that the project will not be jeopardized. One of those sacrificed is McAllen's son (Jimmy Hanley). This action is presented as a moral dilemma, and the film pretends that such sacrifices are inevitable if great scientific works or great ideals are to be realized. But considering the joy with which the financiers took on the project in the first place, you may feel that the dead are victims of the Capitalist system. The film was directed by Maurice Elvey, whose *The Clairvoyant* (1935) is sometimes listed as a film in this genre, concerning as it does a fraudulent mind-reader (Claude Rains), whose powers suddenly and inexplicably become real, making him a celebrity; among his predictions is a mine-disaster – which is fairly spectacular and so much like the similar scenes in *The Tunnel*, released two months later, as to suggest some doubling up.

Balcon's interest in *The Tunnel* may have been triggered off by H. G. Wells's *The Shape of Things to Come*, which had been a bestseller two years earlier. As a philosophical treatise it was unsuitable for filming, but Balcon's* rival, Alexander Korda, invited Wells to write a screenplay based on the material. The first four drafts proved to be unsatisfactory, but Wells's eminence was such that contributions by Korda himself and by Lajos Biro, a frequent collaborator with Korda, went uncredited. The film's director, William Cameron Menzies, returning from Hollywood, also made valuable suggestions at this stage. There were to be further major contributions by the art director, Vincent Korda, by the photographer, Georges Perinal, and Ned Mann & Co., responsible for special effects. The film cost over £700,000, or $1,400,000, more than any other British production to that time, and the result, *Things to Come* (1936) is the first major science fiction movie since *Metropolis* (which, incidentally, Wells particularly despised).

It starts in 1940 in 'Everytown' – which looks like London – with the outbreak of World War II. Three doctors, friends, join the army and two of them have survived when it ends twenty years later – John Cabal (Raymond Massey) and Harding (Maurice Braddell), who returns to medicine, aided by his daughter (Ann Todd) and her husband, Richard Gordon (Derrick de Marney). Doctors are needed, since the survivors of the War are threatened by pestilence, the 'Wandering Sickness'. One man, the Boss (Ralph Richardson), rises to power by sniping at and killing sufferers of the illness. Cabal had settled in Basra, where he had founded 'Wings of the World', an organization for World Peace. By 1970 the world is putting itself to rights, but Cabal is disturbed by the activities of the Boss, 'one of the semi-military upstarts looting and plundering'. The Boss imprisons Cabal, but the latter escapes, with the aid of Gordon, who has become the Boss's chief engineer; and they manage to depose and kill the Boss.

*Except for the war years, when Korda was in Hollywood, these two impresarios produced almost all the worthwile British films (except those produced for Rank by Filippo del Guidice). Korda was more the visionary, but Balcon was responsible for the more lasting body of work, including the Ealing comedies.

Wells is at his best and most ambiguous here, knowing that no matter what the aims of 'peace' organizations, and their methods, they are powerless to prevent war, but *can* create it – though in the event the death of the Boss has no consequence, since Wells was anxious to move on a hundred years. Since we do not yet know how correct were his prophecies about that time, we might pause to say that time has wrecked many of his concepts of the 1940–70 period. It was not difficult to foresee, in 1936, another world war – which Wells imagined in terms of regimented tanks, marching men and black aircraft like bugs. If he did not foresee the age of jumbo-jets (his 'planes are small and with propellers) he did not predict the H-bomb or the cobalt bomb, for who could imagine the unimaginable? The plot of the sequence set in AD 2036 concerns the first rocket to go round the moon: who could have dreamt that that would already have happened over seventy years earlier? In 2036, Massey plays Cabal's descendant, president of this empire or whatever; Edward Chapman, one of his friends in 1940, Passworthy, plays *his* descendant; their children, affianced, plan to be the first people in the moon rocket. A reactionary (Cedric Hardwicke) leads a revolt against the president, but the

The Second World War, as prophesied by H. G. Wells some years earlier in Things to Come.
A fleet of enemy planes – one which anticipates the very look of those which crossed the English Channel in 1940, four years later. **Below:**
The havoc wreaked by an air-raid. Although the bombed city is called Everytown this sequence would have recalled Piccadilly Circus to most of the film's audience.

The moon flight successfully launched in Things to Come. *Its progress is watched by Raymond Massey, at right, as the dictator of the City of the Future, ever more uncontrolled in his ambitions, and Edward Chapman as his aide.*

The moon flight successfully launched in

H.G.WELLS' THINGS to COME

'There are some things man is not meant to know,' says Boris Karloff's mother at the end of The Invisble Ray, *and that is the underlying theme of many science-fiction films, including some in which Karloff appeared. By the time Mama pronounces he (seen at the right) has become a madman, fatally ill, after eliminating any number of his colleagues whom he believes disloyal, including Bela Lugosi (left). His weapon gives the film it's title, but its power comes from a radioactive meteorite, and the movie was directed for Universal in 1936 by the veteran, Lambert Hillyer.*

rocket blasts off and Massey, mad or farseeing or both, makes a speech about conquering the universe, all time and space. This is again Wells at his most challenging, but Chapman, interrupting with 'But we're such little creatures' tends to make audiences laugh today. At the time some found the film risible. Though some critics were awed, others found the film distinctly patchy in effect; the ideas in the plot, not itself of great interest, tend to be quaint. But the world of 2036, as designed by Vincent Korda, Cameron Menzies and presumably Wells, remains to be marvelled at.

While Wells was working with Korda, he persuaded him to film *The Man Who Could Work Miracles* (1936), originally published in 1898. For the production Korda brought from Hollywood the undistinguished German-born director Lothar Mendes, and to play the lead the masterly British character actor, Roland Young. The film begins with a conclave of the gods: one decides to make human beings capable of everything, but wisely decides to start with one man – a draper's assistant, Fotheringay (Young). Fotheringay is at first bemused by his ability to make tables rise or lamps stay lighted when turned upside down. After seeing the shop tidy itself his boss, Grigsby (Edward Chapman), proposes that he put his 'gift' at the disposal of the store – and soon other capitalists are clamouring to put the gift to their own use. A philanthropist (Ernest Thesiger) wants Fotheringay to benefit all mankind, at which point Fotheringay runs afoul of an alcoholic colonel (Ralph Richardson), who tries to kill him. Fotheringay conjures up a palace, with the colonel and the world's leaders packed inside to hear his harangue on the state into which they have brought the world – which, apparently, is to the brink of war. Then – and Wells's imagination was surely crumbling – he stops the earth turning. The palace collapses and the statesmen whirl around in space. As propaganda, the piece is not quite strong enough; as entertainment, one waits for the 'pow' that fails to come. However, the magical construction of the pantheon-like palace and its destruction are remarkable. As with *Things to Come*, the special effects were masterminded by Ned Mann.

Much earlier Mann had worked on the Fairbanks *Thief of Bagdad*. His presence on the Korda lot may be one reason why a new version was put into production, though Mann's name is not among the many people credited, who include three directors, Michael Powell, Ludwig Berger and Tim Whelan. Zoltan Korda, another of Korda's brothers and also a director, and Cameron Menzies are listed as associates, while Alexander Korda himself also directed some of *The Thief of Bagdad* (1940). Filming began in Britain early in 1939 and was suspended on the outbreak of the War. Korda announced that since location filming in Africa was now out of the question, the film would be completed in Hollywood, but the real reason was that his financiers, the Prudential

Although Korda bought the title, **The Thief of Baghdad,** *from Douglas Fairbanks, the two films have little in common but the setting, a flying horse and a magic carpet – which can be seen in the centre of the picture below as it bears the Prince (John Justin) and the Thief (Sabu) who has rescued him from the headsman. That is the Thief again, left, sitting on the ear of the huge djinn (Rex Ingram) who had emerged from a bottle found on a beach. He is a djinn of uncertain temperament, but does help the Prince to come to his rightful inheritance.*

Assurance Company, had decided that they could no longer pour money into what seemed a bottomless pit. Since Korda's first successful film, *The Private Life of Henry VIII*, had proved that British movies could succeed in world markets, the Prudential had been backing him, with no return – partly due to huge overheads and wanton extravagance in the Denham studios which the 'Pru' had built for him. United Artists, Korda's distributors, liked the footage so far shot of *The Thief of Bagdad*, but could only get their backers to take over the project if they could keep tabs on Korda. So this became an American film, eventually being rewarded with three Academy Awards, to Georges Perinal for Colour Cinematography, to Vincent Korda for Colour Art Direction, and to the team that devised the special effects.

Like the Fairbanks film, this is subtitled 'An Arabian Nights Fantasy', but Lajos Biro's screenplay is not otherwise indebted to that. His story has to do with Ahmed (John Justin), the Caliph of Bagdad, who is persuaded by his Grand Vizier, Jaffar (Conrad Veidt), to wander incognito among his people – whereupon he is arrested and decreed mad after being thrown into gaol. There he makes friends with a thief, Abu (Sabu), who helps him escape to Basra, where they make the acquaintance of the princess (June Duprez). Jaffar arrives seeking her hand, and he blinds Ahmed by wizardry before Ahmed can expose him and for good measure he turns Abu into a dog. The princess goes into a sleep from which only Ahmed's kiss can wake her – at which point the story begins, for these events are told in flashback. Among matters to come are a winged horse, a fifty-foot djinn (Rex Ingram), and, of course, a flying carpet. If many of them are spine-tingling, that is because the film is a marvellous combination of special effects, decor and a whopping good story. In my opinion, there are, apart from Disney's early animated features, less than half-a-dozen enduring movies made primarily for children. Three of the others are *The Wizard of Oz*, *The Adventures of Robin Hood* and *The Black Stallion*; this *Thief of Bagdad* is one of the other three.

Although *The Wizard of Oz* (1939) is unquestionably a fantasy it has seldom figured in lists of genre films, perhaps because the story does not need more than a modicum of special effects in the telling. We should, however, acknowledge the flying monkeys belonging to the Wicked Witch of the West, as well as two if not three of Dorothy's companions along the Yellow Brick Road – the Tin Man, the most renowned of all robots, the Scarecrow and the Cowardly Lion. If *The Wizard of Oz* was rapturously received, Hollywood's one genuine science-fiction film of the period was not – *Dr Cyclops* (1940). It was also the first true genre film made in Technicolor, then the only colour system used by the major studios. Paramount produced, and invited Ernest B. Schoedsack to direct, presumably regarding him as an expert on unnatural happenings in the jungle. In this case the setting is Peru, where Dr Thorkel (Albert Dekker) has a laboratory, hidden away in the forest, near a deposit of radioactive ore which provides him with an element that can reduce animals to miniature size. A small group of scientists visit him, persuaded that he needs their help.

They and the guides arrive – only to discover that the egomaniacal scientist merely wants their confirmation of a detail in his experiments. Angry and baffled, they try to wrest an explanation of his work from him. He refuses – and then finds the temptation to experiment on human beings irresistible. They are soon the size of Tom Thumb and in peril from such things as a cat which looks the size of a tiger and an alligator – alarming enough to a normal-sized human being, not to mention a rain-storm which almost drowns them. Eventually they decide that they will only survive if they can kill the doctor. They go for his spectacles first, without which he is almost blind and why confirmation of his experiments was so important. One of them (Thomas Coley) succeeds in smashing one of the lenses; the doctor thus becomes the Cyclops of the title. An arresting moment, observed through a window, shows Albert Dekker lift a cloth from a tray. A perfectly-formed horse, the size of a cat, rises to its feet.

The special effects were admired, with reason, but the film was not. *The New York Times* called it 'an epic of silliness', adding 'In its peculiar way, it is a monument to the ever-expanding universe of the cinema, where, occasionally, anything goes, including flagrant violations of the basic physical and chemical laws, except the still-convenient law of gravitation.'

The time was not propitious to tales of mad scientists experimenting with the laws of nature. A war was being waged in Europe, after several years of fear of a conflict that would engulf the whole world and involve weapons vastly more deadly in scope than in World War I. Although many of the films we have discussed were set in years to come, the only one to consider the future of mankind was *Things to Come*, which envisaged little hope for the human race till the twentieth century was over. Critical estimations of *Dr Cyclops* were little different from those of Universal's horror-cycle, now coming to an end, or the

numerous equally low-budget serials featuring space adventurers filched from newspaper comic-strips, Flash Gordon and Buck Rogers.

Such heroes, along with the many cowboys of B movies, were merely programme-fillers for what the trade called 'the less discerning halls'. Certainly none of the superb leading men of this time – Clark Gable, James Cagney, William Powell – were about to swop their tweeds and three-piece suits for an astronaut's garb, though Ronald Colman journeyed to Shangri-La in Frank Capra's *Lost Horizon* (1936). But Shangri-La, with its age-old truths, was only too much of this earth, even if hidden away in the mountains of Tibet. *Lost Horizon* preached of honour, loyalty and goodness, and the need for such statements seemed needed in the light of the world situation. It said what Hollywood wanted to say on such matters. There came from Hollywood no dreadful warnings like *Things to Come*; the trickery of *The Man Who Could Work Miracles* was more congenial to studio executives. At least, similar japes were offered in the 'Topper' series, produced independently for M-G-M release by Hal Roach. Roach's speciality was comedy, with such practitioners as Charley Chase and Laurel & Hardy, and that was almost certainly what drew him to the novels of Thorne Smith.

The strength of Smith's stories, though often founded in fantastic situations, was their element of spice, though few of his risqué events were likely to pass the censor. Certainly *Topper* (1937) and *Topper Takes a Trip* (1937), both directed by Norman Z. McLeod, seem tame today. Cosmo Topper (Roland Young) is a respectable New York banker, whose friends Marian (Constance Bennett) and George Kerby (Cary Grant) are killed in a car crash. Topper decides to buy their restored, ritzy automobile in an attempt to shock his snobbish, convention-bound, commanding wife (Billie Burke), and the ghosts of the Kerbys take him in hand – getting him drunk and into some embarrassing situations before a pair of Marian's panties finally lands him in court. The second film begins with Mrs Topper in the process of divorcing Cosmo, urged on – nay, ordered, by the much-married Mrs Parkhurst (Verree Teasdale), who takes her off to the Riviera, where divorces are easier. Cosmo doesn't want a divorce, and Marian materializes in order to help him. The third film, *Topper Returns* (1941), directed by Roy Del Ruth and released by United Artists, is an old dark house movie in the manner of *The Cat and the Canary*. Joan Blondell has replaced Miss Bennett as the broad-minded dame whose spectral presence, known only to Topper, will lead him into so many difficult situations.

If those film owed little to Thorne Smith, *Turnabout* (1940) directed by Roach himself is somewhat closer to the original. The subject, again risqué at that time, concerns quarrelling spouses (John Hubbard, Carole Landis) whose wish to be in the other's shoes is granted by the genie in the statue in the bedroom. In the morning he has her voice and she has his. She goes to the office in his body and his clothes, so that everyone, including boss Adolphe Menjou, thinks the worst. He stays at home, where his butch behaviour in her body and clothes nearly lifts Mary Astor's eyebrows

right off her forehead. The film ends with an expected baby gestating in the wrong body. The taste for these films, or at least for the first two 'Topper' films, led Universal to offer *The Invisible Woman* (1941), directed by A. Edward Sutherland – just a year after presenting *The Invisible Man Returns*. *The Invisible Woman* can hardly claim lineage from H. G. Wells, since it is, or is intended to be, a crazy comedy about a model (Virginia Bruce) who answers a newspaper ad inserted by a crazy professor (John Barrymore) asking for guinea pigs. He wants to make her invisible and she accepts, since that gives her the opportunity for revenge on her vicious boss. If Wells used the miracles in *The Man Who Could Work Miracles* as a comment on capitalist greed, Universal uses that on display here as attractive to crooks, who see the advantages of vanishing in order to carry out their misdeeds.

M-G-M's remake of *Dr Jekyll and Mr Hyde* (1941) was planned to reinforce the view, already widely held, that Spencer Tracy was a great film actor – though he himself had to be persuaded to play the role(s) which had brought Fredric March an Oscar. Tracy is superb: as Jekyll, he suggests strange forces at work under the respectable, responsible exterior. As Hyde, he pulled out so many stops that he was accused of barnstorming, but how else, pray, can the role be played? The film postpones our view of the transformation until well into the film, thus creating genuine suspense and building up tension. We have,

Opposite: *A spectral Cary Grant and Constance Bennett in* Topper, *the first feature produced by the Hal Roach Studio, which specialized in comedy shorts though it had produced some full-length comedies with Laurel & Hardy. (In 1984 a subsidiary of the still-active Roach studio announced that it had perfected a method of turning old monochrome films into full colour – and* Topper *was the first film so treated.)*

Above: Joan Blondell in Topper Returns, *with (left) Eddie Anderson and Roland Young.*

King Kong *was so far in the past that this poster makes no reference to its great predecessor. This film is much lighter in tone, but has some bizarre sequences – see the scene on the right.*

however, seen Jekyll's fantasies while the transformations take place, and they are so rich in erotic and masochistic symbolism that one wonders whether Louis B. Mayer understood their significance. They are, today, only too simple to comprehend but were not, I feel, by movie standards then. The director, Victor Fleming, has ensured not only M-G-M's customary production values but those of Stevenson's novel, admirably set out in John Lee Mahin's screenplay. The result, despite some miscasting, is a better version of a Victorian novel than we have any right to expect from Hollywood.

Two other fantasies emerged from Hollywood at the time: *All That Money That Money Can Buy* (1941), directed by William Dieterle for RKO, about a 19th-century farmer (James Craig) who sells his soul to the devil (Walter Huston); and *Here Comes Mr Jordan* (1941), directed by Alexander Hall for Columbia, about a prizefighter (Robert Montgomery) who in a deal with a heavenly messenger (Claude Rains) is allowed to return from death in the body of another. The admiration in which both were held was equalled by that accorded *Flesh and Fantasy* (1943), directed by Julien Duvivier, a three-part film in which either

and Merian C. Cooper
present

GHTY
YOUNG

starring

RE • BEN JOHNSON

STRONG with FRANK McHUGH

RNEST B. SCHOEDSACK

Creator – Willis O'Brien

Play by Ruth Rose

AZING
USUAL!

o Pictures • An Arko Production

circumstances and/or explanations could not be logically contained. Undoubtedly such fantasies appealed to wartime audiences, when the real world was only too horrible to contemplate, be it news from the spheres of battle or the increased pressure of the daily grind. Wartime sentiment dictated the content of *A Guy Named Joe* (1944), directed by Victor Fleming for Metro and one of the prize candidates in the 'M-G-M had no shame' category. Spencer Tracy plays a flyer who is killed, but allowed by Someone Up There (Lionel Barrymore) to return to earth in spectral form to guide his fiancée (Irene Dunne) and encourage her love

for his successor (Van Johnson). The director Stephen Spielberg has announced his intention of remaking this movie. Wartime attitudes also gave new meaning – or so thought Warner Bros – to Sutton Vane's play *Outward Bound*, previously filmed in 1930. Mr Vane proposed a shipload of passengers who gradually realize that they are dead or in the process of dying, their eventual fates to be decided by the Pilot, or Great Divider, when he comes aboard in Act III. In *Between Two Worlds* (1944), directed by Edward A. Blatt, the passengers have become the victim of a bomb on a British port.

Such whimsies were certainly common in French and Italian studios at this time, if without echo of the war, for censorship in both countries was so fierce that few contemporary subjects could be dealt with. Accordingly producers sought refuge in fantasies – stories of ghosts, of people returned from the dead, of hallucinations. Matters were unexplained, unexplainable, unreal and chiefly allegorical. Hollywood continued making films in the same vein, including *Angel on My Shoulder* (1946), directed by Archie Mayo for United Artists, with Paul Muni as a gangster given the chance to return to earth as a judge, and *Alias Nick Beal* (1949), directed by John Farrow for Paramount, with Thomas Mitchell as an honest politician whom the devil (Ray Milland) would like to corrupt. In fact the devil, played by Claude Rains, is a character in the earlier film. Both movies are about political corruption, a subject which had always fascinated film-makers, but since few films on politics had ever been popular it was thought wiser to cloak the message in whimsy. *The Boy with Green Hair* (1948), directed by Joseph Losey for RKO, is an ambitious allegory about a war orphan (Dean Stockwell) whose experiences have left him disturbed and defiant. He is also bald. After he has adjusted, he meets some other war orphans – and finds, the next morning, that his hair, growing again, has turned green. He responds to the ridicule of schoolchildren by saying that his hair is a reminder that there shall be no more wars. The film's statements on war and (racial) prejudice are presented so coyly and with such a sense of self-congratulation that the film did nothing for its cause – nor for the cause of screen fantasy.

The dropping of the first two atomic bombs on Hiroshima and Nagasaki in 1945 had made war even more dreadful to contemplate, followed as they were by the Cold War and the realization that espionage had resulted in the Russians manufacturing their own nuclear weapons. Such matters were too big for the cinema to handle: at least, film-makers doubted whether movies on such themes would have any wide popular appeal. Over much of the world, people were too busy picking up the pieces. Television, before the war a science-fiction dream to most people, became a reality in many homes in the advanced countries; air travel began to replace the ocean liner as a means of getting from one continent to another. And Hollywood gave us *Mighty Joe Young* (1949).

In 1949 *King Kong* was a forgotten curiosity except to those who visited the cheap revival houses, otherwise known as fleapits (the distribu-

In the laboratory is our old friend Dr Jekyll (above) and wherever he is can Mr Hyde be far away? (below). The actor is Spencer Tracy, whom M-G-M's publicity department were describing, not unjustly, as the screen's greatest actor. That was the reason that studio executives forced him, against his will, to invite comparisons with John Barrymore and Frederic March.

tion-exhibition programming then was so organized that it was virtually impossible to see old movies – not that many people wanted to; and those that were beginning to appear on television were of little entertainment value). Joe Young himself is King Kong, or parts thereof – if we assume that Willis O'Brien, the 'Technical Creator', had saved him, or the RKO stores. This was a gathering together of those responsible for Kong – as well as O'Brien, the director Ernest B. Schoedsack, Merian C. Cooper, who produced and provided the story, and Ruth Rose, who wrote the screenplay. Had they continued to love old Kong through the years? Or had they always nurtured the idea of making him a nightclub attraction? For that is what Joe Young becomes, after having been brought from Africa by Max O'Hara (Robert Armstrong), together with the pretty teenager, Jill (Terry Moore), who had brought him up. After Joe has been teased by some trouble-making drunks, he goes beserk, at which point O'Hara realizes his error in taking Joe away from his natural environment. The film's heroes conspire to smuggle Joe out of the country before he can be shot by the authorities, and Joe, sympathetic throughout, becomes a super-hero after rescuing some children from a blazing orphanage. This is an extraordinary sequence, exciting enough but bizarre – if not quite so much as that in which Miss Moore, playing 'Beautiful Dreamer' on a grand piano, is lifted high into the air by Joe. It has been claimed that the film's effects are inferior to *King Kong*, but they are not – though the painted backcloths and matt work are not of the earlier standard.

The film is the link between O'Brien and Ray Harryhausen, who gets a large credit as 'First Technician'. It did not attract much attention, any more than such occasional oddities as *The Beast With Five Fingers* (1946), the tale of a disembodied hand, directed by Robert Florey for Warner Bros. The screenwriter was Curt Siodmak, who worked on this and other tales of the grotesque during the '40s. In 1943 he published his best-known novel, *Donovan's Brain*, which has been filmed three times: as *The Lady and the Monster* (1944), under its original title in 1953, and as *Vengeance* in Britain in 1962 (though that was retitled *The Brain* for American audiences).

George Sherman produced and directed *The Lady and the Monster* with production values no worse and no better than other Republic pictures of the time. Despite that, it is the most rewarding of the three versions, because of the presence of Erich von Stroheim as Professor Mueller, whose dedication to scientific experiment borders, naturally, on the excessive. He has kept alive the brain of a dead industrialist who was murdered: the brain requires revenge and its telepathic qualities are directed towards the professor's assistant, Patrick (Richard Arlen), who finds himself being willed towards more than one murder. He is the monster, and for those interested the lady of the title is the lovely Vera Hruba Ralston, whose film career owed everything to the devotion of the studio's head, Herbert Yates. If moviegoers thought of science-fiction at all, it was of films like this, before returning to the comedies, musicals, Westerns and melodramas that made up the majority of movies offered.

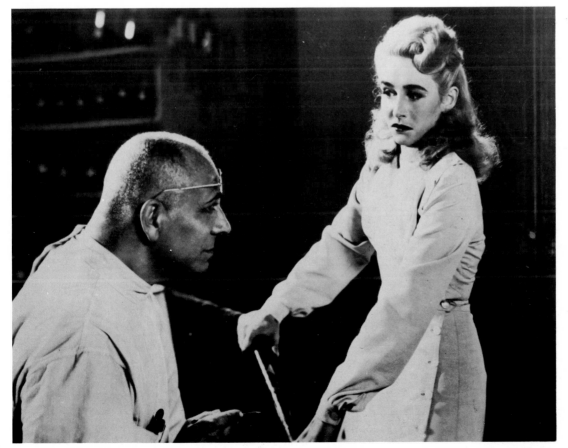

Erich von Stroheim and Vera Hruba Ralston in The Lady and the Monster, *one of the many programmers which were chiefly his lot during his wartime exile from France, where he had maintained his position as a star after Hollywood no longer needed him. He is such a commanding figure in screen history that the world's cinematheques often feature von Stroheim festivals. It took a small San Francisco revival house to do the same for Miss Hruba Ralston – difficult as this may be to believe.*

CHAPTER 3

Anything Is Possible Now

James Mason as Captain Nemo explains the wonders of the Nautilus, and the undersea world, to survivor Paul Lukas. A scene from Walt Disney's 20,000 Leagues Under the Sea.

© Walt Disney Productions 1984

I N 1950 *Rocketship X-M* was launched on an unsuspecting and generally indifferent world. Travel by rocketship was on the verge of possibility, but the film's producer, Robert Lippert, a purveyor of low-budget exploitation movies, was less interested in that than beating George Pal's *Destination Moon* (1950) into the world's cinemas. Among Pal's three screenwriters was James Heinlein, whose *Rocket Ship Galileo*, a children's book, uncredited, was the source of the screenplay. That book, and both films, had their genesis in the scientific discoveries made during the War. It was apparent to both sides in the conflict that victory might be theirs could science be harnessed even more effectively than it was. The Germans developed the pilotless aeroplane, the 'Flying Bomb', launched against Britain in the summer of 1944, a few days after the successful invasion of Normandy, and it was followed some months later by the rocket bomb, invisible to the eye. The United States developed the atomic bomb and dropped two on Japan in 1945, in the belief that that was the only way to prevent the Japanese from fighting till there wasn't another man left. Atomic power was also feasible for peaceful purposes. Experiments continued on nuclear warfare and rocket weaponry when the war was over, in the event of there being another, and the development of radar continued. Radar had been known before the War and had proved vital to the Allies in discovering the whereabouts of German and Japanese aircraft. In 1946 one radar tracking station received echoes from the moon. In 1948 the Hale reflecting telescope was completed at Mount

Movies wondered about the unnatural, the unknown, things to come; but it wasn't till Destination Moon *that they acknowledged the space-age – in a not-very-good film. Compare this spacecraft with the one in* Die Frau im Mond, *on page 33.*

Palomar, California and the first test photographs brought the planets closer. As I have implied, the world in general had other things on its mind, but Lippert and Pal believed that audiences would be interested in the first imaginary journeys to other planets.

Rocketship X-M is destined to land on the moon, but a storm of meteors (in fact, foil-wrapped potatoes) cause it to veer off-course and it lands on Mars (in fact, the Mojave desert in Southern California), where its crew are attacked by mutant survivors of a nuclear war. The guiding force of the film, responsible for production, screenplay and direction was Kurt Neumann, best known (if at all) for some of the later Tarzan pictures and *The Return of the Vampire*, made in 1944. Shooting was accomplished in a mere three weeks, at a cost of $94,000, as opposed to the rival production, which cost $600,000. Neither film was sponsored by a major studio, though *Destination Moon* was produced by Eagle-Lion, which was then owned by the British magnate, J. Arthur Rank. Rank also had shares in Universal, which is why that studio's animation unit contributed the film's supposed documentary, starring Woody Woodpecker, on going to the moon.

The plot of *Destination Moon*, which is minimal, shows how a general (Tom Powers) persuades an aircraft manufacturer (John Archer) to join forces with a space scientist (Warner Anderson) in order to zoom to the moon. The general gets backing from some millionaires after saying 'The country that can launch missiles from the moon can control the earth. That, gentlemen, is the most important military fact of this century,' a rather naive reference to the Cold War. In order to inject action into a static script, there is the possibility of the police preventing the launching of the rocket, since there are no laws governing such a contingency. At the end, the astronauts learn from Control that they cannot return from the moon unless they dump as much stuff – space-suits, furnishings – as possible, and when that isn't sufficient one man elects to make the supreme sacrifice and remain. The moon is pictured as we know it, as are many of the details of the flight (the airless interior of the craft; the walkabout on the exterior). The technical adviser was Herman Oberth, who had served in the same capacity on *Die Frau im Monde*. The director was Irving Pichel, whose uninspired handling make this film hardly more entertaining today than *Rocketship X-M*.

The producer was George Pal (1908–80), whom we should regard as the pioneer of screen sci-fi: it is from his films of the '50s that today's science-fiction epics stem. Born in Budapest, he became a set designer and animator, in Berlin, which he left when Hitler came to power. Working successively in Paris, the Netherlands and Britain he developed his 'Puppetoons', in which stringless puppets – manufactured from a variety of materials including wood and plasticine – were made to move by virtue of stop-motion photography. He moved to Hollywood not long before the outbreak of War in 1939, and in 1941 joined Paramount, whose executives were disillusioned with the cartoonists Max and Dave Fleischer after the failure of their two features, *Gulliver's Travels* and *Mr Bug Goes to Town*. Paramount believed that the

Puppetoons provided a more attractive alternative to the Disney-imitation shorts which were offered by most of the other studios as part of the cinemas' supporting programme. Paramount, however, declined to produce Pal's features, of which the first was *The Great Rupert* (1949), in which Jimmy Durante co-starred with an animated squirrel. The second was *Destination Moon*, which did respectably at the box-office and won an Academy Award for special effects, thus encouraging Paramount to invite Pal back to produce *When Worlds Collide* (1951).

The studio had owned the original novel, by Philip Wylie and Edwin Balmer, since the early '30s, when it had been bought at the behest of Cecil B. DeMille, who intended it to be one of his sermons on man's weaknesses. Instead, he made *Cleopatra*, and the property had languished ever since on Paramount's shelves. Rudolf Maté was engaged to direct, but the cast, headed by Richard Derr and Barbara Rush, did not indicate that the studio had much faith in the project. Indeed, the low budget resulted in unconvincing glass shots, laughable shots of the rocket in flight – and the painted landscape of the new world in the final sequence is both. When the earth is first shaken by turmoil in the universe we see stock shots from old Paramount movies (the fake volcano from *Aloma of the South Seas*, the blazing forest from *The Forest Rangers*, the cliff of snow collapsing, now tinted, from *Spawn of the North*). The plot, which does not exactly compensate for defects elsewhere, concerns panic among scientists when it is evident that two other planets are hurtling towards earth, one to unsettle it and the other to destroy it. With financing from Washington and an evil crippled millionaire (John Hoyt) a spaceship is built, a modern Noah's Ark, which is to take selected human and animal specimens to another planet, along with some encyclopedias. The fact that the rest of the world's population seems indifferent to its fate is another reason why the piece is ineffective.

It is difficult to understand why the special effects won an Academy Award for Gordon Jennings, but this second Oscar to a Pal film was one reason Paramount agreed to produce *The War of the Worlds* (1953), though with a greatly increased budget for the special effects. The cost was $1,4000,000, as against $600,000 for the live action sequences – and that again did not allow for star names. Gene Barry plays a dashing physicist who meets Ann Robinson at the first meeting of the Martians. When Wells published the original novel, in 1898, the telephone was not in general use and the first few automobiles had just been seen on the roads: so that reports of strange things seen in Bromley might be the hallucinations of a madman. As Wells's mystery deepened, it was increasingly clear that the impossible had happened – the Apocalypse had come. When Howard Koch adapted the book for Orson Welles's radio programme in 1938 he reset it in contemporary America, and in such a way that many listeners in the New York area panicked at hearing that Martians had landed in New Jersey. The notoriety of that broadcast had caused all the Hollywood studios to take an interest in the book, but they lost interest with the advent of the War.

The 1938 broadcast was influential in the film's updating of the story and setting it in Southern California. It begins with an explanation of why the Martians decide to invade the earth, whose population believes at first that a meteorite has landed. Undoubtedly alarmed in this shaky Cold War era, the military is as concerned as the scientists – and is needed, for the 'lid' of the meteorite suddenly unscrews, revealing strange, eerie space-craft emitting (in time) mysterious sounds. Those watching are pulverized by the beams wielded by the creatures inside the spacecraft, beginning their rampage of terror. The military solution is to drop an atom-bomb on the Martians' vehicles and perhaps it is not giving too much away to say that the aliens are vanquished by not being immune to the earth's germs; but in the meantime it had seemed that they would destroy all mankind, including – of course – the scientist and his girl, who are hiding in a remote roadhouse.

The director was Byron Haskin, who was reunited with Pal for *Conquest of Space* (1955). Barré Lyndon, who had written the screenplay of *The War of the Worlds*, worked on the adaptation, along with another old hand, Philip Yordan, and George Worthing Yates. The actual screenplay was by James O'Hanlon (fresh from the musical *Calamity Jane*), who had worked on *Destination Moon*. The source was a book by the distinguished scientific writer Willy Ley and illustrated by Chesley Bonestell, the matte artist whose designs had contributed so much to all Pal's science fiction movies.

Bonestell's matte work had also been used by RKO on *The Hunchback of Notre Dame* and *Citizen Kane*; he was also much in demand for the covers of sci-fi magazines, while a huge mural by him may be seen in the Smithsonian Institute. Further proof of the desire for complete authenticiy is demonstrated by Pal's employing Werner von Braun as technical adviser. (Von Braun was regarded as one of the world's leading authorities on rockets, but since he had been responsible for the V-2 bomb before leaving Germany for the US the British would not take fondly to the 1960 film biography, *I Aim at the Stars*). So here is the space-station, the 'wheel' as they call it, which would not become familiar to the vast number of moviegoers till *2001: A Space Odyssey* (1968). Its galley and dormitory foreshadow *Outland*, as does the astronaut who has a sudden attack of mysterious origin while fixing machinery in his space-suit. I mention these later films not as verification of this one's authenticy, but because comparatively few people saw it – with reason, for it is to an extent a rehash of *When Worlds Collide*. The cast is if anything even less interesting; the narrative consists of preparations for the voyage in space, the voyage itself and the arrival, and adventures on the planet.

The time is the 1980s, and there is some tension among the men on the space-station as they prepare to journey to the moon. Its designer is so dedicated that he refuses to allow his son home to visit his wife, while on the eventual journey his dedication leads to insanity and he tries to blow up the craft. Meanwhile, the men watch colour

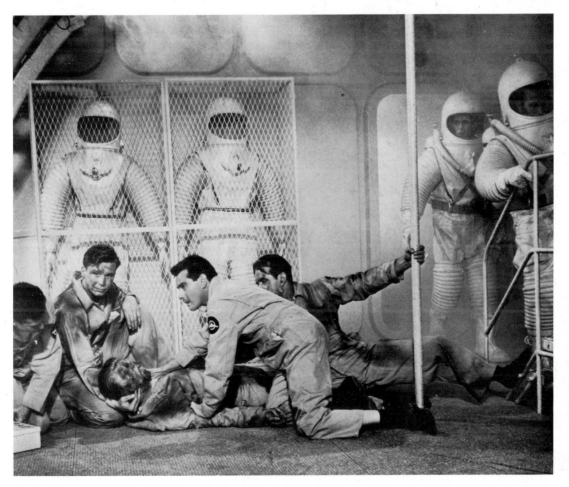

Conquest of Space *was a very grand title for a picture which was not itself overly-ambitious. It also had doubts as to whether space could be conquered without loss to life – as in this scene from the beginning when the mechanism of a space-suit malfunctions.*

television – and Rosemary Clooney in *Here Comes the Girls* is interrupted by the crew's womenfolk in person delivering messages. A Japanese sergeant explains that it's because Japan has few resources that his people live in rice houses – and that is why man must go to the planets, to find new resources for earth. The Supreme International Space Authority decrees that the men are to aim not for the moon but Mars, which turns out to consist of red dust and black rocks. The craft's water system fails, and by Christmas the men are bitter and quarrelsome. A volcanic explosion wrecks the relaunching system, so they are doomed to remain on Mars for ever unless the caves beneath the ship are blasted so that it can be readjusted to a vertical position.

Pal was not the only producer offering genre films, and in fairness to the British film industry, which was not otherwise interested, we should acknowledge that it offered two minor comedies. The first, and better, is *The Perfect Woman* (1949), directed by Bernard Knowles, in which an impoverished playboy (Nigel Patrick) gets a job escorting a female robot – which is impersonated for most of the plot by its inventor's spirited niece (Patricia Roc). *Mr Drake's Duck* (1951), written and directed by Val Guest, concerns an American couple (Douglas Fairbanks Jr, Yolande Donlan) whose ducks reveal one which lays a uranium egg, which puts the cat among the political chickens.

Two major American science fiction movies appeared in the year after *Destination Moon* and *Rocketship X-M*, which might just have created a climate within the industry where any successors were acceptable. But I think that Hollywood's long lack of interest had been jogged by the scientific discoveries being reported in the newspapers. Certainly the press had had a field day with Unidentified Flying Objects or UFOs, which may be associated with the unexplained flying lights seen in the skies throughout history. In 1947 a private pilot flying over Mt. Rainier in Washington had counted nine of these, in disc-like form, to which an enterprising journalist had given the name 'Flying Saucers' – which, having arrived, would not go away and numerous sightings were gleefully reported by the press in the years that followed. Both films, in any case, were based on strong stories, the first allied to mystery thrillers and the second to the 'message' films which crop up from time to time. The first to arrive was *The Thing From Another World* (1951), produced by Howard Hawks and directed by Christian Nyby from a story by John W. Campbell Jr, *Who Goes There*? This may be also said to contain that perennial message – of the danger to scientists of tampering with the unknown. That was ever a familiar theme, going back to Mary Shelley and Robert Louis Stevenson, but this was a fetching, if chilling, variation, as an army unit stationed in the Arctic finds itself unable to cope with an alien – the thing of the title. The unit frees from the ice what they think is a flying saucer and in so doing destroy it; inside they find a huge, unwieldly body which starts on its own rampage of destruction. The scientist at the outpost discovers that the thing is a vegetable that can grow another arm when one is lopped off. It can only be destroyed by electrocution.

Conversely, the alien in *The Day the Earth Stood Still* (1951) wants only to benefit mankind. A space-ship lands in Washington with a messenger (Michael Rennie) and a giant robot. The messenger tells an aide sent by the President that he wants to call a meeting of the world's leaders. Since that isn't possible, the messenger escapes from the hospital where he is being tended and passes himself off as a Mr Carpenter in a suburban boarding house. He is on earth, it turns out, to persuade us to use atomic power solely for peaceful purposes: another war could upset the balance of the universe and if one is threatened his planet would be compelled to destroy the earth. The messenger demonstrates his power by stopping – except for essential services – the world's electricity for a half-hour. Times Square (inundated by the ocean in *When Worlds Collide*) now stands still, as do the Houses of Parliament, the Arc de Triomphe and the Kremlin (the only matte shot of the four). This impressive sequence was one reason for the film's popularity, as were the presence of Patricia Neal, as a fellow-inmate of the lodging-house, and Rennie. Film stars were essential to the success of movies in those days, and this was the only genre film with names. The wooden acting of the generally unknown casts were factors in the general indifference to science-fiction on film; only the one, directed by Robert Wise for 20th Century-Fox, and to a lesser extent Paramount's *The War of the Worlds* were regarded other than as oddities among the cinema fare of this period.

Every so often Warner Bros broke away from the customary bill of comedies, dramas, musicals, thrillers and westerns. *The Beast From 20,000 Fathoms* (1953) may have been inspired by their antique *Lost World*, but more likely its monster-on-the-rampage was suggested by *The Thing From Another World*, inasmuch as the plot doesn't much resemble the credited source, *The Foghorn*, by Ray Bradbury (b. 1920). Bradbury did not like this film, but there worked on it – his first in solo command – Ray Harryhausen, one of his three co-founders on a short-lived science fiction magazine published in Los Angeles in the '30s. Bradbury's story told of a long-surviving prehistoric sea creature who believes that he is no longer the last of his species when he hears what he believes is his mate in the sound of a lighthouse foghorn. Harryhausen was required to make the animal a dinosaur – and one which is revived from the Arctic ice by an atom-bomb test. The creature makes for his old breeding-ground, which just happens to be covered with the skyscrapers of Manhattan. This time Times Square is stampeded by the beast. The director was Eugene Lourié, the Russian-born designer who had done the magnificent art direction for Max Ophuls and Jean Renoir in the late '30s. He would direct two more science fiction movies, *The Colossus of New York* in 1958 and *Behemoth – The Sea Monster* the following year. Like William Cameron Menzies, another great art director, Lourié showed a fondness for this form when permitted to divert from his own job.

Nature struck back at man for misusing the atom in another Warner movie, *Them!* (1954), directed by Gordon Douglas from a story by George Worthing Yates. Something is amiss in

The Thing *itself, in the film of that name, sticking up from the Arctic wastes. And if those guys had known what human – or inhuman – powers it possessed they would have left it there.*

Below: *Another coloured lobby card of a film made in black and white.* The Day the Earth Stood Still *with Michael Rennie and Patricia Neal.*

THE DAY THE EARTH STOOD STILL

MICHAEL RENNIE · PATRICIA NEAL · HUGH MARLOWE

New Mexico. Coupled with some mysterious disappearances are a confusing series of clues – the wrecking of a car and its trailer and a shop; the theft of sugar from both; some gigantic footprints; and a little girl too stunned to do more than point at the desert and say 'Them!' The police sergeant (James Whitmore) in charge of the case welcomes the entomologist (Edmund Gwenn) sent by the F.B.I. when the magnitude of the task is realized. For some ants, set off by 'lingering radiation from the explosion of the first atomic bomb' have mutated into a giant species. Their nest is located and infused with a poisonous gas, but some escape and take refuge in the sewers of Los Angeles. The final message, that man may cause similar breedings if he continues with nuclear experiments, comes persuasively after the subdued, semi-documentary approach; and the film benefits, too, from an above-average cast.

Cameron Menzies himself directed one of his rare films about this time, *Invaders From Mars*

(1953), which begins with the sighting of a flying saucer, arriving on land, by a small boy (Jimmy Hunt). The boy's father, George MacLean (Leif Erickson), is eventually persuaded to investigate and he returns in a zombie-like condition. The mother also changes personality and the boy finds no believers for his story no matter where he turns. But he finds that his parents and indeed everyone has a minute scar in the neck – for the crew of the space-craft have implanted crystalline tablets there, in order to control their minds. After MacLean is discovered trying to murder one of the few people not affected, the boy finds a believer in a newly-arrived doctor (Helena Carter). The Martians are found to consist of giant green-furred androids controlled by a disembodied tendrilled head kept alive in a glass sphere. Cameron Menzies' art direction is more intelligent than the film, which was made too quickly and cheaply to be taken seriously. 20th Century-Fox made it, not as a follow-up to *The Day the Earth Stood Still* but

More inter-planetary invasions, as the title implies, in It Came From Outer Space, *one of the several '50s medium-budget sci-fi movies which owed much to the art directors and the creators of the special effects.*

to cash-in on what was thought to be a box-office stampede for movies in 3-D. In the event, the film was chiefly shown 'flat', and it was so disliked by the studio that it exists in several versions. Most affected by the changes were the endings, which in the American release print shows the boy waking up from a nightmare but then discovering that a flying saucer has landed. . . In the rather longer version seen in Britain the film concludes in a laboratory.

Many of these themes reappear in a much better film, *It Came From Outer Space* (1953), taken from a Ray Bradbury story and directed for Universal by Jack Arnold. An astronomer (Richard Carlson) and his fiancée Ellen (Barbara Rush) see what he thinks is a meteor fall in the Arizona desert. Venturing into the crater he sees what he calls a 'ship', but as is customary everyone else is sceptical. Two linesmen disappear from their trucks, and it is soon apparent that their bodies have been borrowed by aliens wishing to go into town to purchase supplies to repair their craft. They even take Ellen's body. The sheriff (Charles Drake) is eventually persuaded that these are extra-terrestial beings and leads an expedition to destroy them, but the scientist, believing that they stand for peace, sets out to warn them. The film is much more nightmarish than *Invaders From Mars* in turning the real into the unreal, of certainty into uncertainty. There is the implicit threat that we have disturbed the heavens – by war, by examining them too closely – and that they are sending down their creatures to up-end all our beliefs. So often one man stands alone, unable to trust friends and uncertain of the alien and its powers of evil, if so they be.

The handling of *It Came From Outer Space* goes some way in disguising budget restrictions – and the amorphous cyclopean monsters are splendid, especially when we see the transformations from behind their eyes. This was another movie made in 3-D, in which the industry put less faith than in CinemaScope, the wide screen process which was supposed to halt the decline in audiences as people stayed at home to watch television. Only two major films were made in 3-D, the M-G-M musical *Kiss Me, Kate* and Hitchcock's thriller, *Dial 'M' for Murder*. For the most part Hollywood believed that 3-D and sci-fi went together, supported by audiences which liked exploitation fodder. The genre seems to me at its least taking in *The Creature From the Black Lagoon* (1954), also directed in 3-D for Universal by Jack Arnold. I agree with Arnold's claim that the film plays on our basic fear of the unknown, the fear we have of 'what may be lurking below the surface of any body of water'. The discovery of a prehistoric hand brings a party of scientists to a remote part of the Amazon, where they are menaced by something unseen. They conclude that he is amphibious, a fish-man, a survivor of some hiccup in our evolution. So far, so good, and the underwater photography is splendid. I quarrel not that this jungle seems to carry no discomforts, such as bugs or mosquitoes, but that the creature so lacks power: his failure for so long to do more than brush his webbed hand on susceptible limbs is reminiscent of the Silent serials. Nevertheless, there were two sequels also featuring the Gill-man, *The Revenge of*

the Creature (1955), directed by Arnold, and *The Creature Walks Among Us* (1957), directed by John Sherwood.

Arnold had further budget restrictions but infinitely better material with *The Incredible Shrinking Man* (1957), based on the novel by Richard Matheson (b. 1926) which had been published the previous year – and Universal had the good sense to invite Matheson to write the screenplay. Six months after sailing, literally, through what turns out to be a radio-active mist Scott Carey (Grant Williams) finds that his clothes have become too big for him. Medical science can do nothing for him and as he shrinks the press regard him as a freak – as does, in time, his wife, or at least she treats him as if he was a boy. He loses his job and is later found living in the doll's house his wife has bought – and prey to the family cat, once so loved and now so feared. These sequences are some of the most spine-tingling in cinema, and there are others equally good towards the end,

The Creature From the Black Lagoon, *in the film of that name, and looking really rather endearing in this shot – which may be why the film's makers keep him hidden so long from its characters, who are constantly being terrified by a brush of its hand against arm or leg.*

A poster for one of the best genre films of this period. Audiences may have found it 'A fascinating adventure into the Unknown', but 'fascinating' would not have been the adjective used by the unfortunate hero.

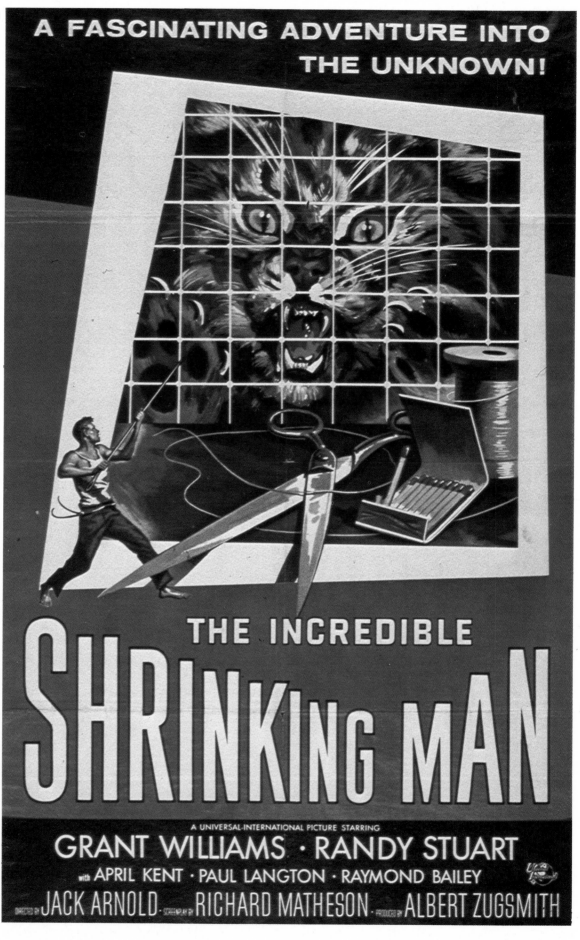

when Carey is battling a spider with a needle or floundering under a tempest-like torrent from a water-pipe. He is deserted by all, for his wife and brother believe him to have been the cat's dinner, but his spirit rises to the occasion. The growth of Carey's courage in inverse proportion to his size, is a theme better handled than the implications of the early symptoms and becoming a world celebrity. Matheson's story deserves more detailed, expensive treatment, but the 1981 remake was a fiasco. For the record, *The Incredible Shrinking Woman* was a vehicle for the comedienne Lily Tomlin, who played a suburban housewife reduced in size by being too lavish with detergents while cleaning her home.

Hardly one of these films – and there were others, less significant – offered concepts or ideas not hinted at before 1950, which we should now regard as the prehistoric age of the sci-fi movie. Those earlier films went unseen except by the members of film societies. As far as audiences were concerned the science-fiction film began in 1950. Apart from the belief that the space-age was imminent (which it wasn't in *Things to Come*) the

most salient advance over earlier films was the belief that man's tampering with science led to strange mutations and either the emergence of vehement primevals or the advent of hardly less friendly planetary creatures. It was Walt Disney (or his advisers) who returned to sources. In filming Jules Verne's *20,000 Leagues Under the Sea* (1954) he kept it firmly in the 19th century. He also utilized a first-rate cast and allocated a huge budget – at $5 million, more than that of most of these movies put together. This one starts in 1868 with rumours that a mysterious monster is destroying shipping in the South Pacific. An armoured frigate goes to investigate and is rammed by the monster, which turns out to be the submarine *Nautilus*. Three survivors, a marine biologist (Paul Lukas), his aide (Peter Lorre) and a harpoonist (Kirk Douglas) become the prisoners of the submarine's embittered captain, Nemo (James Mason). Nemo has made amazing scientific discoveries but will not pass them on to a world which had wrongfully imprisoned him and taken his wife and child. So he lives here under the sea or in an island headquarters. True to Verne, Nemo

Walt Disney's 20,000 Leagues Under the Sea, *his first excursion into science-fiction, was a shot in the arm for the genre, for it was the first in many moons to have first-class production values all along the line – and the first with major stars. James Mason (as Captain Nemo) plays the mighty organ in his study within the* Nautilus *in* 20,000 Leagues Under the Sea.

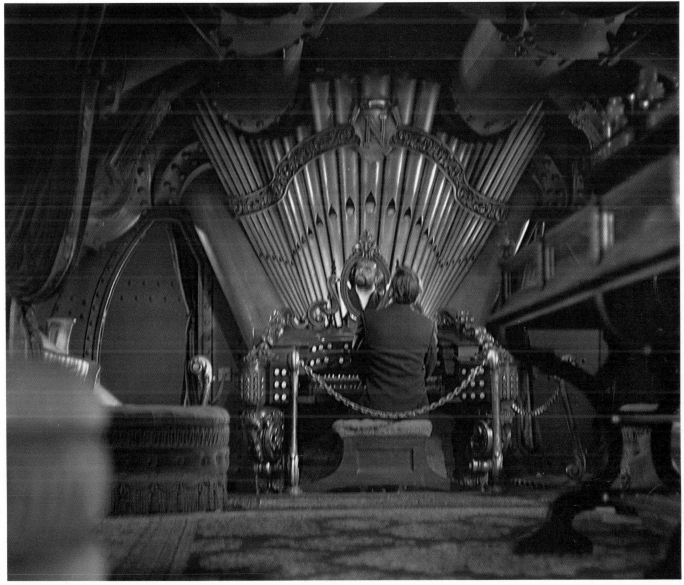

Kirk Douglas on the defensive against a giant squid in 20,000 Leagues Under the Sea.

wrecks ships to prevent geological materials from reaching a civilization which will create wars with them. But his final message, with a clear reference to the atom bomb, comes across merely as banal. Indeed, Earl Fenton's screenplay is elementary, and the direction by Richard Fleischer – son of Disney's old rival, Max Fleischer – so uninspired that even such a fine actor as Mason can only make Nemo, a fascinating character in the original, of middling interest. (But at least this film doesn't invent a past for him or incorporate chunks of *The Mysterious Island* as did Universal's primitive and seemingly interminable 1916 version). The film's triumph is in art direction, for which John Meehan won an Oscar. Especially notable is the *Nautilus*, both its 19th-century baroque exterior and the captain's red plush salon.

The huge box-office success of Disney's film was the first confirmation offered to Hollywood that audiences would support science-fiction. It was both the first Disney feature and the first sci-fi movie in CinemaScope. Although the wide screen was being used indiscriminately by some companies (especially 20th Century-Fox, which owned the patent to CinemaScope, though there would soon be rival systems) it was unsuitable, for instance, for intimate comedies or domestic dramas. Used intelligently, it enhanced musicals, historical epics and Westerns. M-G-M, encouraged by the popularity of *20,000 Leagues Under the Sea*, decided to make a sci-fi spectacle. Since this was M-G-M, entering the world of science-fiction for the first time, *Forbidden Planet* (1956) was given a large budget, colour and CinemaScope – and although the stars, Walter Pidgeon and Anne Francis, were hardly in the first league, they were a further guarantee of the film's respectability. It

may be supposed, however, that M-G-M's decision to enter this new field was the knowledge that the screenplay was an exceptionally strong one. It was written by Cyril Hume from a story by Irving Block and Fred M. Wilcox, who also directed. Wilcox made only a few films, of variable quality, including *Lassie Come Home* and an excellent version of the children's classic, *The Secret Garden*. The initial premise is taken from Shakespeare's *The Tempest*, inasmuch as a middle-aged wise man (Pidgeon) and his daughter (Miss Francis) are joined on their 'island' by some travellers. The strangers are astronauts, who arrive – we are in the 21st century – on the planet Altair-4 to reconnoitre and if possible discover the fate of a spaceship which disappeared years before. Dr Morbius, the wise man, and his daughter Altaira turn out to be the sole survivors. The rest of the crew were apparently murdered. Morbius survived and digested the learnings of the Krell civilization, which became extinct aeons ago. 'Prepare your minds for a new scale of scientific knowledge, gentlemen' says Morbius to his visitors as he shows them the vast palace of technology left by the Krell. Then one of the spacemen is found dead: the wild beasts which roam the planet are harmless, but there are mysterious forces around – and one appears, like a ferocious Muppet, in outline only. 'Doc' (Warren Stevens) resolves the mystery as he too is dying: the Krell had unleashed enormous reserves of power, but they had forgotten one thing – the 'Monsters of the Id', beasts which can be summoned from the subconscious. Without knowing it, Morbius had used them to kill the other members of his spaceship, and they have begun to reappear because he dislikes the intruders. Says the

Following Disney, M-G-M produced a genre film of top quality, Forbidden Planet, *though Walter Pidgeon, right, was no longer a great box-office attraction – and certainly the astronauts (Jack Kelly, Warren Stevens, Leslie Nielsen) were interchangeable with the rather wooden actors cast in parts like these in most of the other, and lesser, films of the period. That is Robby the Robot in the forefront of this scene.*

commander (Leslie Nielsen), 'We are all monsters from the subconscious, that's why we have laws and religions.' Partly because the astronauts are as zombie-like as those in the other space movies of that time, the film has longueurs; but the sci-fi movies of a generation later are prefigured by the playful robot, Robby, who waits on Altaira, and the almost mystical banks of technology. Presumably Arthur Lonergan, credited with Cedric Gibbons (overseer of all Metro's art direction) was responsible for the latter. A team from Disney created the monsters, which could still terrify young spectators.

The film was moderately successful, but did not for the moment encourage M-G-M to attempt anything further in the genre. The studio did, however, give backing to George Pal for his long cherished version of the Grimm fairy tale, *Tom Thumb* (1958), originally planned in 1939 as a Puppetoon feature to rival Disney. Since *The Wizard of Oz*, if not before, M-G-M had had much success in making films for the younger members of the audience, which may be why Pal approached the studio after Paramount vetoed the project. It must be said that this was not one of the better ones, with pallid humour and pretty-pretty decor. The worst misfortunes of Tom (Russ Tamblyn) never approach those of the incredible shrinking man, but the trick photography is virtually impeccable. Pal turned director with this film, and though he wasn't especially talented in that direction *The Time Machine* (1960) is one of the more memorable of the genre films of this time. As with *Tom Thumb* the special effects, masterminded by Pal, won an Oscar, but they are unequal in quality. And as with *The War of the Worlds*, Pal simplifies and trivialises many of

Above: Tom Thumb – *or as the ads always had it,* tom thumb – *with the dancer Russ Tamblyn in the title-role, being watched by the Queen of the Forest (June Thorburn), who started the whole thing off by presenting him to the childless woodcutter and his wife. She's also allowed a romance of her own, with Tom's friend Woody, played by Alan Young.*

Left: *Having left* The Time Machine, *in the film of that name, Rod Taylor is involved in some derring-do which probably would not have met the approval of H. G. Wells, who wrote the original novel. Does Taylor know of the figure behind him? It's not clear from his expression.*

Wells's intentions, removing the dire prophecies and historic parallels. Particularly to be regretted is the excision of that conflict, both Darwinian and Marxist, between the Eloi and the Morlocks, representing the obedient, hardworking proletariat and their effete rulers. These have become respectively a young blond race, existing without books and without feeling, and some underground bogey men, for whom the Eloi sacrifice themselves. This part of the film is conventional sci-fi swashbuckling – with trimmings which may have inspired Pierre Boulle to write the novel later filmed as *Planet of the Apes* (1967). Otherwise, David Duncan's screenplay is both intelligent and imbued with a spirit of adventure. Rod Taylor is the host late for dinner, in 1895, because he has taken a journey in the fourth dimension – that is, in time, in the machine he has invented, a Victorian contraption based on the common or garden armchair. His trip shows the skies racing past, the seasons, the flowers, with a stop in 1917, another during the Second World War and a third in 1966, after which come earthquakes, to bury the time machine and its travellers for centuries till another upheaval restores them to the light. That is when the time traveller becomes involved in the affairs of the Eloi, and we might wish him back in his seat.

M-G-M allotted only a small budget to Pal's next production, *Atlantis, the Lost Continent* (1961), and the result, with crude models and footage borrowed from *Quo Vadis?*, must have had that studio's proud founders spinning in their graves. Pal was no luckier with *The Wonderful World of the Brothers Grimm* (1962), M-G-M's co-production with Cinerama, or with *Doc Savage – The Man of Bronze* (1975), based on a comic strip, which he produced for Warner Bros. His other two late productions are, however, of interest, even if the first is hard to 'place'. *Seven Faces of Dr Lao* (1964)

was based on a novel by Charles G. Finney first published in the '40s and entitled *The Circus of Dr Lao*. That the ideas in the novel bear some resemblance to those in the 1983 film of Ray Bradbury's *Something Wicked This Way Comes* (published in 1962) is no accident: Charles G. Finney and Ray Bradbury are one and the same. The setting is a small Western town whose inhabitants are being persuaded to vacate it by a powerful cattleman (Arthur O'Connell). Trying to expose him is the crusading newspaper editor (John Ericson), who finds an unexpected ally in an elderly Chinaman, Dr Lao (Tony Randall), who arrives in town with his circus and magic powers. At least, he appears to the editor in the guise of Merlin, and after failing to provide magic for the expectant crowds he does appear in other guises – including, we may suppose, a giant dragon, even if we had seen it grow from his pet fish. The make-up artist, William Tuttle, was the first in his craft to receive an Academy Award – deservedly so, for he designed some remarkable creations for Randall's seven faces. The printed credits list one of these as the god Pan, but in this case praise is not due to Tuttle, for the publicity stills contradict the credits by identifying Pan as Ericson – as the sharp-eyed spectator may have guessed. Pan appears to the editor's girl friend (Barbara Eden) playing and dancing so seductively that she breaks out in a cold sweat. This is an extraordinary sequence to be found in a Hollywood movie of the time, though its implications would presumably be lost on young audiences. Otherwise the special effects are better than competent, even if they include some inserts from *Atlantis, the Lost Continent* (including its borrowings from *Quo Vadis?*).

Pal's last film for M-G-M was *The Power* (1968), directed by his old collaborator, Byron Haskin and scripted by John Gay from the novel by Frank M.

Atlantis, the Lost Continent is one of the last to date of many motion pictures devoted to the age-old myth (probably based on fact) that there once existed a large block of land in the Atlantic Ocean. Most of those movies ended with the inundation of Atlantis, in this case caused by fire and volcano – due to evil scientists tampering with natural forces. The film also chronicles the adventures of a poor Greek fisherman lured to Atlantis by its Princess, who had somehow got lost at sea.

Here are two of The Seven Faces of Dr Lao, *with (below) Barbara Eden and (left) with Arthur O'Connell. Tony Randall played Dr Lao, the Chinese showman able to magically transform himself, with the aid of some remarkable make-up. Clearly it isn't Randall with Mr O'Connell but some form of puppet, but the other still is confusing, for Dr Lao certainly looks like Randall. Other publicity pictures identify the god Pan as John Ericson, who plays another role in the film – but who would appear to be doubling for Dr Lao in this particular sequence.*

Robinson. Its theme is the conflict between two researchers at the California Institute of Space Technology: one, Nordland (Michael Rennie), is our old friend, the being with plans of world domination, and the other, Tanner (George Hamilton), is the one who gradually begins to realize that that is his aim, and that he is using murder to achieve it. Nordland moves stealthily, not wanting to show his hand, for he kills by telekinesis and he has to remove Tanner, who possesses the same power – but is unaware of it. Nordland is also ignorant that his potential rival is Tanner, which is why he kills indiscriminately. And when he does discover that Tanner threatens him, he retaliates by making him a non-person for those technicians still alive. This may well suggest some confusion (why doesn't he just direct his telekinesis towards Tanner?) in the script and the film is unsatisfactory: but this is the first film on this theme, to become so common in the late '70s. So it may be acknowledged that Pal pioneered yet another sub-section of the genre movie.

One other producer, then equally unlauded, was specializing in sci-fi movies, Charles H. Schneer (b. 1920), though their low budgets and derivative plots contributed to their being disregarded by all but the most diehard sci-fi fan. *It Came From Beneath the Sea* (1955), directed by Robert Gordon and part-written by George Worthing Yates, tells of an octopus (though there was only money for five tentacles), mutated into a monster by an atomic test, which destroys the Golden Gate bridge; *Earth vs. the Flying Saucers* (1956), directed by Fred Sears from a story by Curt Siodmak, part-written for the screen by Yates, shows aliens descending from their spacecraft with designs on Washington's monuments; and *Twenty Million Miles to Earth* (1957), directed by Nathan Juran, warns of the awful consequences of interplanetary travel, for the astronauts returning from earth have brought back from Venus an egg which, when hatched, reveals a reptilian humanoid which grows into a monster determined to destroy Rome. The story of this last-named, and the special effects of all three films, were done by Ray Harryhausen – and his special effects, considering the (financial) means at his disposal, are remarkable.

These films went unreviewed except by the trade press, and they were booked into cinemas specializing in exploitation fare. Given the blanket disregard of the industry élite, Harryhausen's devotion to his metier is admirable. It may well be said that that was all he could do or wanted to do, but he was keeping alive the cinema's capacity for fantasy.

His predilection for the old myths was first apparent in *The Seventh Voyage of Sinbad* (1958), produced by Schneer and directed by Juran. Sinbad (Kerwin Mathews) has a fiancée (Kathryn Grant) who is reduced to Tom Thumb size by an evil magician, and she can only be restored to full size by Aladdin's lamp, which is on the island of Colossa and protected by a menagerie including a dragon, a huge cyclops, a multi-armed snake woman, some two-headed rocs and a duelling skeleton. In *Mysterious Island* (1961) some Americans and two British ladies encounter giant crustaceans, and giant birds and bees. This remake of

the Jules Verne story was directed by Cy Endfield and made in Europe, with Columbia distributing worldwide. Schneer and Harryhausen found it cheaper to operate from Britain, and with backing from Columbia they produced a lasting body of work – though it went critically unnoticed at the time. We shall look at some of their later films in another chapter.

In fact, *Mysterious Island*, like *The Time Machine*, was triggered off by Disney's *20,000 Leagues Under the Sea*, which led to *Around the World in 80 Days*, a version of Jules Verne that was one of the most acclaimed and popular films of the decade. These two movies had convinced the industry that there was a huge market for fantasy-adventure, preferably if set during the last century. Of the cycle that followed, the best is easily *Journey to the Center of the Earth* (1959), directed by Henry Levin for 20th Century-Fox. The screenplay was by Charles Brackett and Walter Reisch, whose recent films lacked the wit of some of the great ones to which they had contributed twenty years earlier (with Billy Wilder they had written *Ninotchka*). They certainly responded to Verne's tale, as have the art directors – for although there are process shots, back-projections and some where you can smell the papier-maché there is imagination to compensate. James Mason plays a scientist who becomes excited on being given a piece of rock from Iceland, for it contains elements only otherwise found on Mount Etna. He decides that an underground passage links Iceland to Sicily and in leading an expedition he comes across a forest of giant mushrooms, an underground sea and the lost city of Atlantis, not to mention assorted perils of villainy and treachery.

Among those impressed was the producer Irwin Allen, who remade *The Lost World* (1960) with Fox as distributor and himself as director and co-writer, with Charles Bennett. The resemblances to *Journey to the Center of the Earth* are manifold, but where that was tongue-in-cheek this is only too po-faced, though unintentionally funny in a crass way. The magnified iguanas posing as prehistoric animals worked in the earlier film, but here they are merely pathetic. The plot is neither true to Conan Doyle nor the 1925 version: Willis O'Brien, the progenitor of that, is credited here with 'technical effects', whatever they may be, and perhaps because he refused to be associated with the 'special effects'. It was his last film, and we might wish him after all his fine work to have had a more worthy exit.

While Hollywood played with the science-fictions of the past, the small splutter of futuristic tales almost petered out entirely. Apart from *Conquest of Space*, already noted, there was only one notable movie about interplanetary travel in the second half of the '50s, *This Island Earth* (1955), directed by Joseph Newman for Universal. Unfortunately, it offered only an uninspired rehash of the quintessential sci-fi story as churned out in the specialist magazines for over two decades. As such, perhaps we should look at it at length, while noting that it has all the faults of the bad sci-fi movie, including wooden acting, painted planetary settings and mayhem with monsters and ray-guns. There is even a longish section in which the stone-faced hero and his vaguely comic side-

One of the Ray Harryhausen creatures, at the right, which have delighted moviegoers now for more than two generations. It is threatening Kerwin Matthews, at the far left, and the film is The Seventh Voyage of Sinbad.

Intrepid explorers on the Journey to the Center of the Earth, *based on Jules Verne's novel. They are, from left to right, Peter Ronson, Pat Boone, Arlene Dahl, and James Mason as the leader of the expedition, giving a tongue-in-cheek performance which more than compensated for the inadequacy of some of the other players.*

Much of This Island Earth *takes place on the planet of Metaluna, which, as can be seen, hardly has a hospitable air.* **Below:** *Rex Reason and Faith Domergue are about to visit it, at the behest of one of its inhabitants, Jeff Morrow, the standing figure on the right of the photograph.*

kick indulge in meaningless laboratory experiments. That hero is Cal (Rex Reason), doctor of science, involved in the industrial development of atomic energy. Above Los Angeles, his plane turns green as he loses control; in the lab strange things, like condensers, start turning up. He assembles a kit which has arrived from nowhere, to find himself watching a screen, from which a man calling himself Exeter (Jeff Morrow) tells him that he is wanted for a special scientific mission: and then the machine auto-combusts. Cal travels to what he supposes is Georgia, to a scientific conference, but most of the others attending appear to have been brainwashed. Exeter confesses that he is only a mouthpiece and that he is from another planet, Metaluna, desiring only that these clever men go there as slaves to help it out of its difficulties. With a colleague, Ruth (Faith Domergue), Cal tries to escape, but they are pursued by killer rays emanating from the sky. Exeter rescues them and promises them safe-conduct for their voyage to Metaluna. It seems that Cal has made important discoveries in the use of uranium, which the Metalunians need in order to defeat the unnamed forces trying to destroy them. The surface of the planet has been almost wholly destroyed, causing its inhabitants to dwell underground; as Cal and Ruth are touring the tunnels they encounter a mutant – a manlike creature with a head like a fly – who is one of a race, Exeter explains, developed to act as slaves. The mutants turn out to be hostile, and we have to suppose that they have been suborned by the enemy. They try to prevent our heroes from returning to the spacecraft and there is even one stowed away. . .

Much of this is nonsense, as written by Franklin Coen and Edward G. O'Callaghan from the novel by Raymond F. Jones, but they clearly worked with glee. The film, though only competently directed, conveys the thrill of people who have loved pulp literature. Many of its elements had never before been seen in a movie, while its account of interplanetary warfare prefigures those of the present day. It is of more value than the one serious drama of the future, *On the Beach* (1959), in which an atomic fall-out has caused the death of most of the world's population. It has not yet reached Australia, so that is where most of the film takes place, as the characters talk glumly of the end. The Australians queue up meekly for their suicide pills and Ava Gardner says 'It's so unfair. I didn't do anything. . . You know what I want to do? Walk down the rue de Rivoli.' The issues raised by this film, written by John Paxton from the novel by Nevil Shute, are overwhelming and are better left alone than handled mawkishly and portentously. Its producer-director, Stanley Kramer, was fond of message movies, but this one could convert no one to the cause of nuclear disarmament.

Population is also doomed in *Invasion of the Body Snatchers* (1956), though this film lacks the pretensions of *On the Beach*, centering on some strange

Very few of the science-fiction movies of this era received much advance publicity or much attention from the press. Those, however, who cared for the genre, immediately recognized Invasion of the Body Snatchers *as a probable classic. Beware those giant pods, which are not what they seem.*

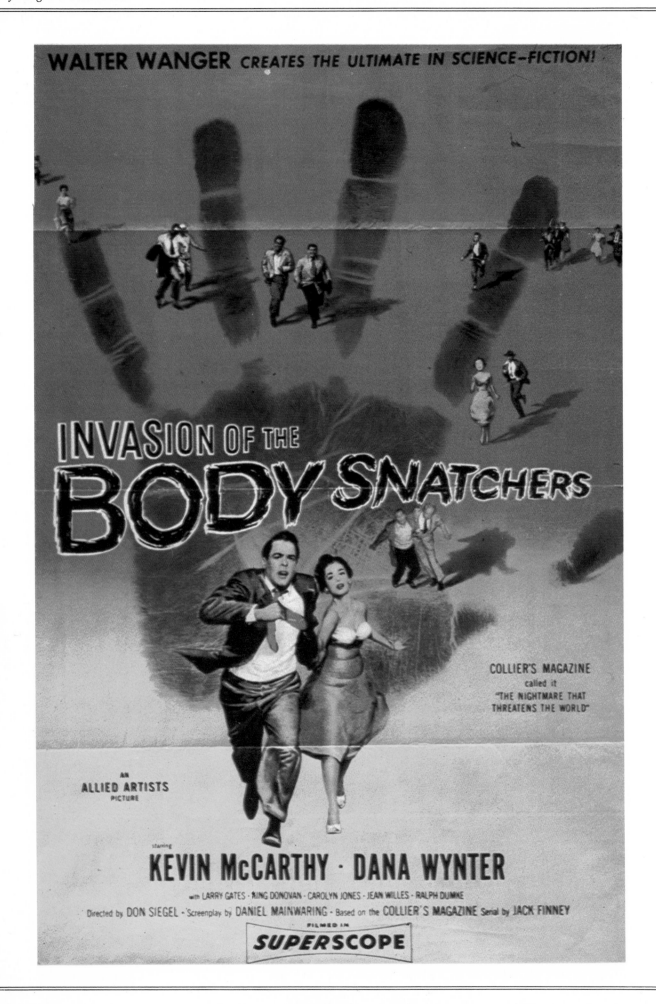

happenings in a small Californian town. A doctor (Kevin McCarthy) finds people waiting to see him who then change their mind; others report relatives undergoing personality changes. A writer friend (King Donovan) finds a body on the billiard table, but one without fingertips and as they watch the face begins to assume the writer's own aspect. In a greenhouse they discover four giant pods opening, and inside bodies are forming – their bodies. Gradually they realize that these things are taking over the bodies of the townspeople, and those so captured are hostile zombies. The writer succumbs, and he and some others guard the doctor and his girl friend (Dana Wynter), knowing that they must eventually fall asleep and then can no longer resist transformation. Daniel Mainwaring wrote the screenplay from a *Collier's* magazine serial by Jack Finney, which was recognized by the producer, Walter Wanger, and the director, Don Siegel, as an allegory on McCarthyism, when conformity became more important than principles and fear contributed to people losing their humanity. The careers of neither of them were at their peak, though they were not necessarily affected by their left-wing views. Wanger had produced some memorable films in the '30s and '40s, but had been shunned by most of the industry for shooting at the man he believed to be his wife's lover. Siegel had graduated to potboilers after some major features at Warners – and he would make his finest films in the late '60s and early '70s (e.g. *Coogan's Bluff*, *Dirty Harry*, *Charley Varrick*). It is an eerie story, but it is Siegel's grasp of narrative which is paramount in making the film such a compelling one. He shot, chiefly on location, in only eighteen days. Sci-fi addicts recognized the film as one of the best offered yet in this new genre, but it was only to find a wide audience on revivals.

One reason for the slow acceptance of such horror and fantasy stories was that for most people the future was as depicted in George Orwell's novel *1984*, in which the world is governed by totalitarian regimes denying – or at least forbidding – individual thought and emotion. Orwell wrote a satire; as a socialist he was alarmed by the conformity demanded by the Soviet rulers and their satellites and by the growth of bureaucracy after the election of the Labour government in Britain in 1945. In 1954 BBC television transmitted a dramatized version of the novel which caused such a sensation that it was repeated some weeks later – and both transmissions were live. Because of the brouhaha, the second was put on tape for a third airing and a film version was made for cinemas, in 1955, directed by Michael Anderson. The producer brought over two American stars, Edmond O'Brien and Jan Sterling, in the hope that the movie would create as much stir in the US as the BBC's version had done in Britain. But the screenplay was misconceived; the result was as grim as the novel, without being either as telling or harrowing. It failed to attract many people into seeing it.

BBC Television was also responsible for widening the public's interest in science-fiction, by virtue of the serials written by Nigel Kneale (b. 1922), a former actor. *The Quatermass Experiment* (1955) had been televised two years earlier and this film version suffered from the usual budget restrictions on genre movies – despite the arrival of yet another American, Brian Donlevy, again in the hope of duplicating in the US the popularity of the original six-part serial. Donlevy plays Professor Quatermass, designer of a spacecraft which is the first to explore the heavens. It has crashlanded on returning, and only one astronaut (Richard Wordsworth) has survived. In hospital it is discovered that he has an undiagnosable disease, with an organism in his arm which is simultaneously eating him away and multiplying as it mutates into something resembling a cactus. In order to survive it must eat, and to eat it must kill, reproducing and growing all the while till this mass, once a man, is hoisted on some scaffolding on Westminster Abbey, with dissolution into a million other organisms imminent. Val Guest directed for Hammer and wrote the screenplay with Richard Landau. Kneale himself worked with Guest on the script of *Quatermass II* (1957), again based on a BBC serial transmitted two years earlier. In this case the professor (Donlevy) discovers that a remote government research installation has been taken over by aliens from another planet, who have assumed the bodies of the workers while acclimatizing themselves to their new environment. The film does not have the impact of the earlier one, and once again one wished that Kneale's vivid material had been given the more expensive treatment it deserved.

The film company, Hammer, had not long changed its name from Exclusive, which had begun less than ten years earlier, originally specializing in cheap movie versions of BBC radio serials. The success of the two Quatermass films paved the way for Hammer's entry into the international market, though after the even greater popularity of its *Dracula* in 1958 it specialized in tales of horror. So although *Quatermass and the Pit* (1968) had been televised in the winter of 1958/9 it did not reach the large screen for ten years. Kneale wrote the screenplay; Hammer permitted the use of colour for the first time and assigned the direction to Roy Ward Baker, a film-maker with some more substantial credits than Guest. Even so, Kneale's imaginative force is so strong that it deserves an equally powerful approach in the handling. There is an immeasurable gain in the casting of the bearded Andrew Keir as Quatermass, a more convincing professor than Donlevy, while James Donald is quietly impressive as Dr Roney, an archaeologist called in to help him.

During excavations at a London Underground station (it is being enlarged) some unusual prehistoric remains have been exposed. The further discovery of a rocket-like object brings to the scene a bomb disposal expert, Colonel Breen (Julian Glover), who believes this to be a relic from World War II. But Quatermass is of the opinion that it has its provenance in an extra-terrestrial invasion. The object resists a drill, but a hole appears in one side, which shatters to reveal large locust-like creatures, long since dead. Research reveals that this particular place has been associated with evil since the Roman era, so that Quatermass begins working on the theory that the creatures are Martians who came to earth in an attempt to perpetuate their race when it seemed doomed to

Nigel Kneale wrote two
science fiction serials for
television which were so
successful that they were
later filmed — on higher
budgets than the BBC
could then afford, but
perhaps still inadequate to
the imaginative quality of
Kneale's work. An
American star, Brian
Donlevy, was brought over
to head the cast in both
movies, and here he is, as
the professor for whom both
films are named.

Above: The Quatermass
Experiment, *with David
King-Wood as the doctor
and Richard Wordsworth
as the astronaut who has
returned from space with an
undiagnosable illness, and*
(**right**) Quatermass II. *In
the US the films were
retitled respectively* The
Creeping Unknown *and*
Enemy From Outer
Space.

extinction on its own planet. Five million years ago they would have found apes, which they programmed, or genetically 'improved', thus starting 'mankind' on its upward path – a theory which arouses the wrath of a government Minister, indignant at the inference that we owe the human condition to the intervention of *insects*. The insect invasion may be seen on television of sorts, for the rocket has retained its power and the doctor's assistant (Barbara Shelley) is able to receive its recorded images. Indeed, the craft had been propelled by mental power which had been stored all these years – and thus, disturbed, is able to project into the night-sky a huge locust-like figure, its horns reminiscent of those associated with the Devil in Christian mythology. The popul-

ation of London, not surprisingly, is disturbed, and people near the site begin attacking each other; a repetition of what happened on Mars five million years before, when its inhabitants started slaughtering each other to prevent mutations.

I shall not reveal the final twists of the story, but the reader will already have realized that it is prodigal with ideas; and it is the first film to send science-fiction backwards in time, with the suggestion that the evolution of mankind owed much, if not everything, to the intervention of aliens. The ten years between this movie and its BBC serial presentation would see an upsurge in the number of genre films produced, but none with such resonance or so many concepts central to what science-fiction is all about.

Quatermass and the Pit, with Andrew Keir, at the far right, as Dr Quatermass – and much more convincing than his predecessor in the role.

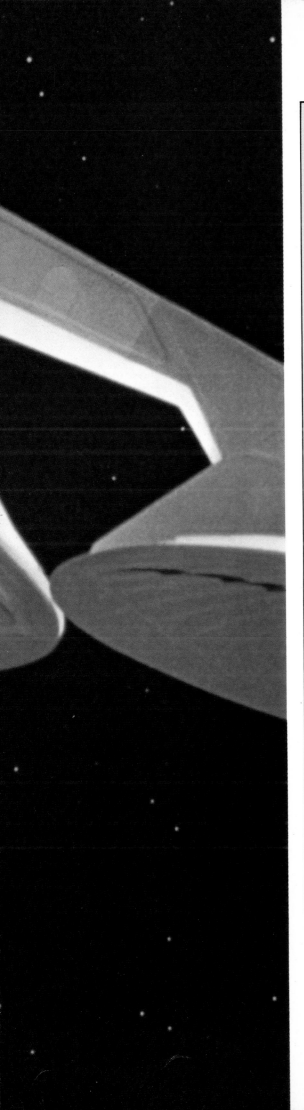

CHAPTER 4
Man In Space

The world of space, as memorably created in Stanley
Kubrick's 2001: A Space Odyssey. On the voyage to
Jupiter one of the astronauts, Gary Lockwood, takes a
space walk to investigate trouble.

In Village of the Damned *(below) Barbara Shelley and George Sanders, right, begin to suspect that there is something abnormal about their son, Martin Stephens. And they would be right. The idea was developed in the less successful sequel,*

Children of the Damned *(bottom) but the children in this case came not from one village but from six different countries – and here they are, escorted by Barbara Ferris to London to be studied by experts.*

B y the early '60s movies had become frequent programming for television and many revival houses had become art houses, showing vintage and foreign-language films. So by this time most interested buffs would have seen *Metropolis*, *King Kong* and *Things to Come*. The landmarks since what we may call the revival in 1950 were less apparent, and unless you were a hardcore science-fiction fan you could hardly have guessed that *Invasions of the Body Snatchers* was superior to *I Married a Monster From Outer Space* (1958). Neither title, after all, is particularly attractive. But since so many movies of the latter's poor quality prevented the genre from being taken seriously we might glance at it briefly. Gene Fowler directed from a screenplay by Louis Vittes, which starts with Bill (Tom Tryon) about to marry Marge (Gloria Talbot). Returning from his bachelor party he sees a body on the road; getting out of his car, he feels faint as he sees a strange creature and a cloud of smoke. During the honeymoon a bolt of lightning reveals strange patterns on his face. A year later Marge feels that Bill isn't the man with whom she fell in love, a view doubtless strengthened when he strangles the dog she has bought as an anniversary gift. We had seen a friend also transformed into a cloud of smoke, and when he turns up there is hostility between the two men till lightning reveals that he too has patterns on his face. Then, when one policeman hits another over the head it is clear that he, like Bill and friend, has been taken over by aliens. That, anyway, is the start – for with laughable dialogue and derisory special effects the piece is unwatchable.

Paramount produced, so here is another example of a major studio reckoning that sci-fi was for the throwaway end of the market. Although most critics wrote enthusiastically about the first two *Quatermass* films they were released as double-bill features, and though we may point to their relatively low budgets and unimportant sponsor, Hammer, it is true that the larger companies were uncertain as to whether audiences could be attracted to cinemas to see stories that they had recently seen free on their home screens. Science-fiction remained unrespectable, whatever status had been achieved by Verne, Stevenson and Wells, and more recently *1984* and Aldous Huxley's *Brave New World*. In the US the novels of Ray Bradbury were beginning to find readers beyond addicts of the genre and the same was true in Britain of those of John Wyndham. Wyndham's reputation was such that we might have expected the film versions of his novels in the early '60s to be impressive. A number of reasonably important talents were involved; but the results show only too clearly the industry's uncertainty about science-fiction.

Village of the Damned (1960) is the better of the two, and not only because of the greater fidelity to its source, *The Midwich Cuckoos*, as written by Sterling Silliphant and George Barclay with Wolf Rilla, who also directed. One day an English village and its inhabitants are immobilized, but investigations reveal no reason. When, two months later, twelve women are diagnosed pregnant, they are unable to explain why. The six boys and six girls that are born are all physically alike, with flaxen hair and disturbingly sombre eyes. By the age of nine they are intellectually superior to those around them, with telepathic powers of communication between themselves which lead, the villagers suppose, to the deaths of two men hostile to them. The 'father' of one child, a physicist (George Sanders), is admitted to their trust and he realizes that they are alien half-breeds who must be eliminated before they are able to carry out their plan to multiply. The film has tension, achieved by stealth rather than pyrotechnics, but the appearance of the children is telling. A sequel, *Children of the Damned* (1963), based on the same source material and directed by Ben Arbeid, concerns several similar children brought from all over the world to be studied by UNESCO. It is less effective than the earlier film, both of which were regarded by the distributor, MGM, as at best double-bill fare.

The Day of the Triffids (1963) rated colour and wide screen, unlike *Village of the Damned*, but budget restrictions are only too apparent elsewhere. It starts at Kew on a night of meteorites, which have a strange effect on a triffid plant, causing it to move, grow and strangle a night watchman. An American seaman (Howard Keel) removes his bandage after an eye operation to find London in chaos and everyone blind – except one small child (Janina Faye), who decides to cross the Channel with him after hearing on the radio of an international conference to be held in Paris. A subplot concerns a couple (Kieron Moore, Janette Scott) on a lighthouse. They haven't gone blind, which is odd, for there seems nothing to do there but watch the meteorites responsible. By this time the triffids are on the rampage, affected – we now know – by plant spores radiated from outer space. One of these lethal plants attacks the couple on the lighthouse, having presumably wafted across from land, and although when attacked it multiplies the couple discover that sea-water kills the triffids. With that matters are summarily wound up, and not too soon in view of some of the dialogue, such as the brisk response of one lady, suddenly blinded, on learning that the seaman and the little girl are sighted; 'Oh good, I do hope you'll stay and help us.' Philip Yordan, who wrote and directed this travesty of Wyndham's novel, had done distinguished work in the past. His director was Steve Sekely.

If the prospect of aliens (or anything else) arriving here from space remained happily remote it was the reverse where humanity was concerned. The possibility of man flying through the heavens came a step nearer when the Russians successfully launched their Sputnik in 1957, and in 1961 the Soviet astronaut Yuri Gagarin became the first man in space by orbiting the earth in just under 90 minutes, at a maximum speed of 17,560 miles per hour and a maximum altitude of just over 203 miles. It was now only a matter of time before man landed on the moon, and it was a matter of pride, prestige and glory for whoever reached it first, the Russians or the Americans. It was in this climate that Paramount decided to produce another movie about space travel, but when it came to the actual launching the studio got cold feet. *Robinson Crusoe on Mars* (1964) was not presented as the rather special film it is, and indeed in Britain it was released with almost 30 minutes cut. It may have been believed that the public would not support a movie with virtually one character and Paul Mantee was unknown. As far as I can discover he hasn't made a film since, but he carries this film without difficulty. He plays the sole survivor of a spacecraft which falls out of orbit trying to avoid a UFO, with only a pet monkey for company. 'But here's the hairiest problem on Mars,' he tells it, 'isolation.' After arriving he had settled down and prepared to die. Then he discovers that he can filter oxygen from

Not as spine-chilling as all that. But this lurid, somewhat unimaginative poster does not betray the quality of the product.

If the scene looks familiar it's because the tale has been subjected to many interpretations, including pantomime and several previous film versions. That is Crusoe (Paul Mantee) with Man Friday (Vic Lundin), and if you didn't know you could probably guess the title, which is Robinson Crusoe on Mars.

the burning rocks; and he follows the monkey, which leads him to food of sorts, and water. Once assured of survival, he sets out to collect scientific information for the day he is rescued. There is a magical moment when Crusoe, as I'll call him, finds the skeleton of a man's hand in the gravel, and a scary one when a man's shadow is revealed as that of his supposedly dead colleague, now a zombie. One day Crusoe rescues an alien, the object of a laser beam attack from a spacecraft. At first he believes the creature dumb, but when he finds that he can speak he teaches him English – and christens him Friday. Friday tells him that his attackers will return, able to trace him – no matter how far underground he goes – by the metal bands on his wrists, so these must be sawn off as the men and the monkey flee through the subterranean passages.

As long as the images stick to the rocks in natural colour (much of the filming was done in Death Valley) they are fine. They are not so terrible with coloured lights trained on them, but the rocks and mountains are back-projected against hideously coloured skies which sometimes contain the least convincing spacecraft since the old serials. For all that, much of the movie is genuinely eerie, as directed by Byron Haskin from a screenplay by John C. Higgins and Ib Melchior, the last-named a frequent contributor to genre films at the lower end of the scale.

Absolutely at the other end is *Dr Strangelove: or How I Learned To Stop Worrying and Love the Bomb* (1964), set in the near future and concerning the future after that or, rather, the necessity of

preserving it, for events have been set in motion which can lead to the end of the world. This was 'a nightmare comedy', according to its producer-director, Stanley Kubrick, who wrote the screenplay with Terry Southern and the author of the original novel, *Red Alert*, Peter George. General Jack Ripper (Sterling Hayden) has convinced himself that there is a 'Commie' plot to demoralize the free world by fluoridising the water, and he therefore sets the permanently-circulating fleet of B-52s on course for a nuclear attack on the Soviet Union. As he explains to his RAF liaison officer, Mandrake (Peter Sellers), Clemenceau once said that war was too important to be left to the generals but that was no longer true, since politicians have too much to think about to bother about a really important thing like war. Ripper commits suicide, but Mandrake finds himself in the equally lunatic care of Colonel 'Bat' Guano (Keenan Wynn), while in the Pentagon the American president (also Sellers) is thwarted at every turn by General Buck Turgidson (George C. Scott), who quotes the rule-book to him *ad nauseum*. Turgidson knows the book; it is all he knows. He is not sure – the book offers no guidance – that Ripper has not performed a service for humanity or at least the American part of it. 'The man is psychotic,' says the president mildly. 'I'd like to wait to comment on that till all the facts are in,' replies Turgidson. 'I will not go down in history,' says the president, 'as the greatest mass-murderer since Hitler,' and Turgidson has a brilliant riposte to that, 'Mr President, sir, I think you should be concerned with the American people, not your

Left: *The War Room in Dr Strangelove, with Peter Sellers, in profile, at the right, immediately beneath the lights, and George C. Scott, top centre. This is Sellers in one of his three roles in the film, that of the American president. The film itself, a chilling comedy-drama about a possible Third World War, did much to make science-fiction acceptable to the film industry.*

Below: *Dr Strangelove and Peter Sellers again – but this time in the title-role. The film was not, incidentally, in colour.*

image in the history books.' As the inevitable happens, these two are discussing with a scientist, Strangelove (Peter Sellers in the third of his roles), the possibility of preserving important specimens of humanity, such as military men, underground till the fall-out has worn off in a hundred year's time. *Dr Strangelove*, in fact, is less about the dangers of nuclear war than those of the mentalities of the people who control our destinies.

The film is a brilliant, satiric, provocative parable, whereas *Fail Safe* (1964), which came along a few months later, merely warns – sometimes simplistically and novelettishly, as written by Walter Bernstein from a bestselling novel by Eugene Burdick and Harvey Wheeler. The title refers to that system which limits American nuclear operations and the plot concerns that moment when it fails, due to a mechanical error, and two pilots journey on towards Moscow to eject their bomb. There is a discussion as to whether American forces should shoot down one of their own planes, as if there were any doubt that two lives should be sacrificed to save millions.

It is not clear why the president (Henry Fonda) doesn't suggest to the Russian leader – he spends most of the time on the hot line – that he order the plane shot down, nor is it clear why the men do not turn back when the president orders them to do so. They have apparently been warned that any verbal instructions could emanate from an interpreter, which seems a foolish alibi, while the ending, far from being apocalyptic as in Kubrick's film, is merely ghastly. The president orders a similar bomb to be dropped on New York in order to convince the Russians that the first bomb was an accident. The director, Sidney Lumet, has handled the tale in sombre and urgent fashion, giving it more credibility than it deserves.

It is doubtful whether Kubrick or Lumet regarded these two films as science-fiction, but both men were (and remain) among the world's leading film-makers. Very few practitioners in the genre carried as much prestige. That fact, and the popularity of *Dr Strangelove*, created a more favourable attitude in the industry for tales of the future. Two equally admired young French film-makers, both members of the *nouvelle vague*, made their contributions – Jean-Luc Godard and François Truffaut. Truffaut had been trying to get backing for a film of Ray Bradbury's novel *Fahrenheit 451* since making his name with *Les Quatre Cents Coups* in 1959, but the projected cost was too high to attract a backer in France. Universal's British outfit agreed to finance it, partly because of *Dr Strangelove* and partly because Truffaut was regarded as an economical film-maker: his friend and colleague, Godard, had recently demonstrated that it was possible to make a 'quality' sci-fi film on a low budget with *Alphaville, Une Etrange Aventure de Lemmy Caution* (1965).

Alphaville, supposedly a typical city of the future, consists of seedy hotel rooms of the kind familiar to anyone who has tried to tour Paris with the minimum means, existing incongruously beside massive, modern high-rise buildings. These have been photographed by Raoul Coutard in a harsh, cold manner as to indicate a place of no individuality or feeling, a city where technology reigns, where public executions – the victims are men who have behaved 'illogically' – are held in the swimming baths. Unsurprisingly, Alphaville is controlled by a computer. This announces near the beginning of the film that reality is sometimes so complex that it can only be transmitted by legend. The reality of this movie is fear of the technological future, while the use of Lemmy Caution, a hero of the pulps – played here as before on film by Eddie Constantine – is Godard's explanation of the sort of level he is using: that fear is expressed through a square-jawed tough guy who thinks only after he has acted. In the plot he calls himself Yvan Johnson, a reporter from *Figaro-Pravda*, who has travelled across intergalactic space to Alphaville. In truth, he is Agent 003 of *les Pays Exterieures*, and he is trying to track down Harry Dickson, a predecessor, and Professor von Braun. Dickson, said to be in the tradition of Dick Tracy and Flash Gordon, turns out to be a blubbery old man (Akim Tamiroff) kept going on booze and girls supplied by the administration. Professor von Braun pretends that his name is Nosfératu, but Caution sees through

EDDIE CONSTANTINE

ALPHAVILLE

UNE ÉTRANGE AVENTURE DE LEMMY CAUTION

JEAN-LUC GODARD

AVEC
ANNA KARINA
ET
AKIM TAMIROFF

MUSIQUE DE
PAUL MISRAKI

DISTRIBUTION ATHOS FILMS

him; his daughter Natasha (Anne Karina) has already become Caution's guide and companion, but she is also a robot. The computer is another of the professor's inventions, which must be destroyed if Caution is ever to escape.

The borrowed names give an indication of the sources plundered. Godard always was audacious, and he has stolen recklessly – from Orwell, from Cocteau's *Orphée* (like Eurydice, the heroine is bidden not to look back), from Ian Fleming, from the cartoonist Saul Steinberg. His own touches are sometimes amusing, such as the hotel maids who supply tranquillizers without asking –

as well as themselves – and are accordingly labelled 'Séductrice' of *deuxième* or *troisième* class. But as so often with Godard the proliferation of ideas is not always consistent with clarity, and we might prefer to see the citizens of Alphaville go beserk instead of merely being told about it.

Godard's future society nevertheless is more convincing than that of Truffaut, whose *Fahrenheit 451* (1966) founders on its script, written by him and Jean-Louis Richard (and presumably rendered into English, which Truffaut then knew imperfectly, by David Rudkin and Helen Scott, credited with the additional dialogue). Bradbury's concept

The title, Fahrenheit 451, *refers to the temperature at which paper burns. Julie Christie as the girl who, an unrepentant reader in a repressive society, turns the hero's mind in a new direction.*

*Cyril Cusack (left) and
Oskar Werner in*
Fahrenheit 451. *Cusack
as the fire chief warms his
hands over burning books;
Werner's expression
suggests that his job as a
fireman is rather less than
satisfying to him now.*

of a future society which banned and burned all books was perhaps suggested by what happened in Nazi Germany, and certainly the film presents a fascist society. Books have been replaced by television and wordless comic-strips. A house without a television aerial is special, which makes the television owners jealous, so that the books inside must be rooted out and burned. Now that houses are fire-proof that job is done by the fire brigade. The police chief (Cyril Cusack) is contemptuous of novels, and books in general 'make people want things they never had', which makes him reject philosophy. The argument stops there, without mention of microfiche or the learning necessary for any society which needs architects, scientists, engineers and doctors. The hero is Montag (Oskar Werner), a fireman, who realizes how terrible his job is after meeting a girl (Julie Christie). After reading a book, he becomes an addict. He begins to regard his wife (also, disconcertingly, Miss Christie) as a vapid creature, sprawled before the television set. He reads her David Copperfield's account of his marriage to Dora, but the film does not delve into this disintegrating marriage. The characters are lay figures, and the ending, when Montag joins the book-people in their hide-out, is curious instead of chilling. And many of the anomalies of this future society are foolish: Montag's electric razor is thrown away because 'the very latest thing' is a cut-throat razor. After this film came out young men were growing sideburns, moustaches, beards and long hair in a way that had not been fashionable since the 19th century and Victorian patterns became fashionable for women. Anything considered essential to elegance might return to favour but not, surely, something as dangerous as a cut-throat razor.

Another French film-maker, Roger Vadim, turned to science-fiction with *Barbarella* (1968), also made in English for world audiences. Barbarella is a 40th century astronaut who first surfaced in book form in 1964, but she was better known for her risqué adventures in a comic strip. Her creator, Jean-Claude Forest, is listed as the film's artistic consultant, and he is one of several writers who worked with Terry Southern on the screenplay. This begins with Barbarella (Jane Fonda) being instructed by the President (Claude Dauphin) to go in search of Durand-Durand, who has left Earth with the world-shattering Positronic Ray. She crash-lands on a planet where two little girls set their man-eating dolls onto her, but she is rescued by Mark Hand (Ugo Tognazzi), who insists on making love to her. Love on earth had become a matter of exaltation-transference pills and psycho-cardiograms, so she enjoys this experience. Hand helps her move to another planet, populated by outcasts from the city of Sorgo, including a crazed professor (Marcel Marceau) and a gentle, blind angel, Pygar (John Phillip Law). The professor repairs Barbarella's space-ship, while Pygar carries her in his arms to Sorgo, where she is welcomed by the bisexual queen (Anita Pallenburg). The queen tries to have Barbarella pecked to death by budgerigars, but Barbarella escapes, due to the machinations of a revolutionary (David Hemmings) who owns a vast aray of machines, few of which function properly. Eventually Barbarella meets the object of her quest (Milo O'Shea),

disguised and demented, and with a plan to master the universe. Although the special effects are good, the only element of this movie which most people liked was the tongue-in-cheek performance of Miss Fonda, who has based her characterization on another comic strip, 'Little Annie Fanny' in *Playboy*. She was then married to Vadim, whose talent was not for satire, which is what the script was intended to be. Dino De Laurentiis and Paramount had backed it because of the scandalous reputation of the comic strip and because the public had shown a brief interest in the genre as camp entertainment.

This was because of a television series, also based on a strip cartoon, *Batman*, so outstandingly popular that a digression is required on the super-heroes of the strips. The first of these was Buck Rogers, who had first appeared as Anthony Rogers in Philip F. Nowlan's *Armageddon – 2419*, published in *Amazing Stories* in 1929. The National Newspaper Service syndicate commissioned Nowlan and cartoonist Richard Calkins to create a strip, and *Buck Rogers in the 25th Century* first appeared in 1929. A radio serial of the same name began in 1932 and two years later a rival syndicate, King Features, came up with *Flash Gordon*. The Olympic Gold Medallist, Buster Crabbe, played both heroes for Universal in four serials made between 1936 and 1940 – three times as Flash and once as Buck, though the episodes of all four are virtually interchangeable.

As Buck hopped from planet to planet in his future millenium another writer, Lester Dent, conceived the idea of someone similar to help the FBI – without its knowledge – crush the bootleggers and gangsters who were front page news. Accordingly *Doc Savage* made his debut in the magazine bearing his name in March 1933. This physical and mental giant, financed by his gold mines in South America and aided by his assistants, the Amazing Five, fought crime – this was the heyday of the American gangster – from his secret laboratory and skyscraper penthouse. His friends thought him merely a successful surgeon, hence the 'doc'; his Christian name was Clark, and it was in homage to him that Superman's earthly moniker was Clark Kent. *Superman* was the invention of Jerome Siegel for *Action Comics*, whose first number appeared in June 1938. Superman's popularity was such that the publisher, National Comics, featured another such, *Batman*, whose adventures were first seen in *Detective Comics* in May 1939. The difference between them was that while Superman is an alien masquerading as a man, Batman is a human being, a millionaire whose true identity is known only to his valet and to his nephew, Robin. He had vowed to fight crime after his parents had been killed by gangsters, and under his mansion is an elaborate laboratory as well as a garage housing the Batmobile.

Doc Savage remained unknown except to his original admirers, till George Pal produced a movie, *Doc Savage – Man of Bronze*, which was a quick flop on its release in 1975. But Superman and Batman, once conjured up, refused to die. *The Adventures of Superman* was a radio serial from 1940 to 1953, when its hero moved over to television for a further four years. From 1941 till 1943, when

Barbarella looked, at the time, like yet another example of '6os kitsch, and might profitably be studied by anyone taking an historical interest in such matters. It is also of note in showing Jane Fonda in her brief period as sex goddess before becoming a very fine serious actress.
Right: *With David Hemmings, the revolutionary to whom she owes her escape from the wicked Black Queen (Anita Pallenburg).*
Below: *Presumably helped by the prayers of the Angel, (John Phillip Law), Barbarella captures her adversary.*
Opposite: *Milo O'Shea is Durand Durand, for whom she has been searching throughout the universe, all of which he covets for himself.*

Buster Crabbe as Flash Gordon, fearless and resourceful hero of the strip cartoons, who featured in three movie serials in the '30s and '40s. This scene is from the last of them, Flash Gordon Conquers the Universe (1940), *also known more modestly as* Peril From the Planet Mongo *and/or* The Purple Death From Outer Space. *Flash's old adversary, Ming the Merciless, has managed to create from the planet Mongo the Purple Death, an epidemic spreading throughout our world and part of his plan to conquer the universe. Can Flash prevent him from achieving his object?*

he left Paramount, Max Fleischer produced seventeen animated shorts featuring Superman. In 1943 Columbia produced a 15-episode serial called *Batman*, whose production values made Universal's Flash Gordon and Buck Rogers series look positively luxurious. All of them were intended for the most undemanding audiences, and Columbia tried again, on derisory budgets, as the demand for serials disappeared entirely – *Superman* in 1948 and *Batman and Robin* in 1949. Gene Wright, in *The Science Fiction Image* calls the 1943 Batman 'undoubtedly one of the worst serials ever made', adding that it was re-edited and issued 'with great success' in 1965, as *An Evening with Batman and Robin*. That presumably is the reason why the television series that began the following year was notable for the camp elements. It was an immediate sensation, playing as a cliffhanger on ABC twice weekly and attracting such artists as Ethel Merman, Joan Crawford, Vincent Price, Tallulah Bankhead and Eartha Kitt to play the comic villains. As Wright says, 'Batmania passed quickly', and after being cut back to one night the following season the programme was dropped in February 1968.

It leaves as residue a movie designed to cash in on the furore, *Batman* (1966), 'dedicated to fun-lovers everywhere' – and therein lies its trouble, for the jokiness becomes tedious. And since Batman does not have superhuman powers there is hardly the chance for the special effects of the later Superman movies. There are wrinkles in the sky, though a real sea has been superimposed on it; when Batman and Robin climb a wall they are only too clearly walking before a camera turned at right angles; the shark biffed with the batgun is only too palpably stuffed. Cloaked and masked in their ridiculous outfits, the Dynamic Duo can only be wooden; but Adam West is pleasant enough in his few scenes as Bruce Wayne – the millionaire whom the Catwoman (Lee Meriwether) is trying to kidnap, in the obviously vain hope that they can capture Batman when he tries to rescue him. The Catwoman, The Penguin (Burgess Meredith), The Joker (Cesar Romero) and The Riddler (Frank Gorshin) – all villains from the television series – are plotting to control the world. That is why they have captured the Commodore (Reginald Denny) – because he has invented a ray, the Dehydrator, capable of reducing people to piles of dust. The scenes involving the ray are the only ones which truly link this movie to science-fiction, and it isn't very enjoyable, as directed by Leslie H. Martinson. It does, however, represent the television series which, though a nine-days-wonder and deliberately comic, did continue to widen the audience for this form of fantasy.

20th Century-Fox, which co-produced and distributed, put considerable resources into a serious genre movie, *Fantastic Voyage* (1966),

Adam West as Batman *in the 1966 movie of that name. Only his valet and his cohort Robin know the real identity of Batman – that of the young millionaire Bruce Wayne. Here's Batman in his laboratory, deep below Bruce's palatial seashore mansion.*

Fantastic Voyage, *and the picture below shows events happening inside the body of the gentleman on the operating table in the picture on the right – which is why the voyage was fantastic. Among the voyagers miniaturized to the size of pinpricks (or something like that) is Stephen Boyd, seen at the right of the lower illustration.*

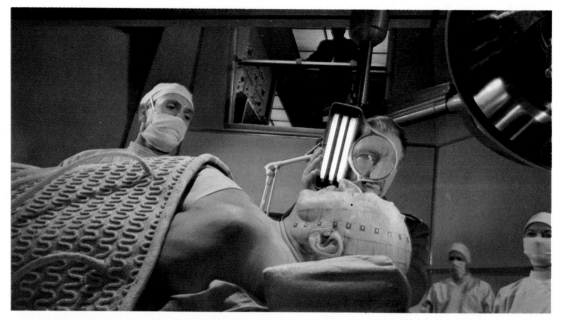

though that was based on a premise so outlandish that you might be forgiven for also thinking it high camp. A defecting Czech scientist is injured in a car crash after arriving in New York, and it is decided by the military that a group of people will be shrunk small so that they can be injected into the body of the scientist in order to effect a cure from the inside. The film, though otherwise effectively directed by Richard Fleischer, fails at the crucial point – showing us the 'submarine' and the crew being reduced. And for most of the time we are watching the craft floating or flying through plastic with what looks like globules of oil around it. The predominant colour of the plastic is not red, as you might expect, anything but. The craft eventually reaches the brain after several mysterious attempts at sabotage, engineered, we finally learn, by that member of the crew who is a Communist at heart. The cast includes Edmond O'Brien, Donald Pleasance, Arthur Kennedy and Arthur O'Connell, but the two top-billed players, Raquel Welch and Stephen Boyd, are as wooden as any of their sci-fi predecessors.

You may feel the same about Charlton Heston in *Planet of the Apes* (1968), also produced by 20th Century-Fox, but he was probably the biggest box-office star so far to lend his support to a science-fiction film. And Franklin J. Schaffner, though his reputation has somewhat dimmed, was then considered the equal of Kubrick or Lumet. Heston, however, is ideally cast as an astronaut – one who with his colleagues moves through a time warp before crashing their craft in the sea near an incredible landscape ('doubled' by national parks in Utah and Arizona). The three survivors travel far before they find signs of life, in the form of some subhuman form of man. These creatures turn out to be the slaves of apes, whose hostility to the astronauts results in one being killed and another dying during surgery. Because man is considered destructive, the survivor, Heston – temporarily deprived of speech – is put in a cage; and the apes chatter about science. Leon Shamroy photographed all this magnificently, and Schaffner gets the utmost from the eerie situations. The make-up (for the apes) and the special

effects are of outstanding quality; but the latter part of the picture is hardly better than old B movies, as Heston escapes, with the help of two sympathetic apes (Kim Hunter, Roddy McDowall) and the inevitable girl (Linda Harrison) from the nearby human tribe. At the end Heston finds the Statue of Liberty buried in the sand, and he shrinks to his knees shrieking 'Maniacs!' with all the artificial anguish of which he is capable. This cry echoes the end of *The Bridge on the River Kwai*, a smooth, modish anti-war film based on a novel by Pierre Boulle, though the cry there ('Madness!') was not in the book. *Planet of the Apes* is also based on a novel by M. Boulle, clearly indebted to the screenwriter of the earlier film. The writers of this one, both admired talents, are Michael Wilson and Rod Serling.

The film was so successful that there were four sequels, *Beneath the Planet of the Apes* (1970), directed by Ted Post; *Escape From the Planet of the Apes* (1971), directed by Don Taylor; *Conquest of*

the Planet of the Apes (1972) and *Battle for the Planet of the Apes* (1973), both directed by J. Lee Thompson. Heston has a guest role in the first of these, which is almost as powerful as the original; the law of diminishing returns applies to the others, all of which combine action-adventure with warning of the consequences of nuclear warfare – though this last element disappeared from the short-lived television series of 1974.

Public acceptance, early in the year, of *Planet of the Apes*, was an encouraging sign to the executives of M-G-M, then in the midst of a series of upheavals, who were worried about the cost of *2001: A Space Odyssey* (1968). The approved budget of $4,500,000 was already high for a genre with only isolated box-office successes – and that had escalated to $10,500,000 during production, which lasted almost a year longer than originally estimated. M-G-M presumably took heart from the rushes and the reputation of the producer-director, Stanley Kubrick. Kubrick also wrote the

Left: *A scene from* Planet of the Apes, *showing those creatures pursuing (human) astronauts who have accidentally invaded their habitat. The picture opposite shows the make-up used for the apes, who had many human characteristics. You may just recognize that fine actress Kim Hunter, who appeared – if that is the word – in several of the sequels, which included* Beneath the Planet of the Apes (below). *James Franciscus, upper right, is a captive of the mutant humans.*

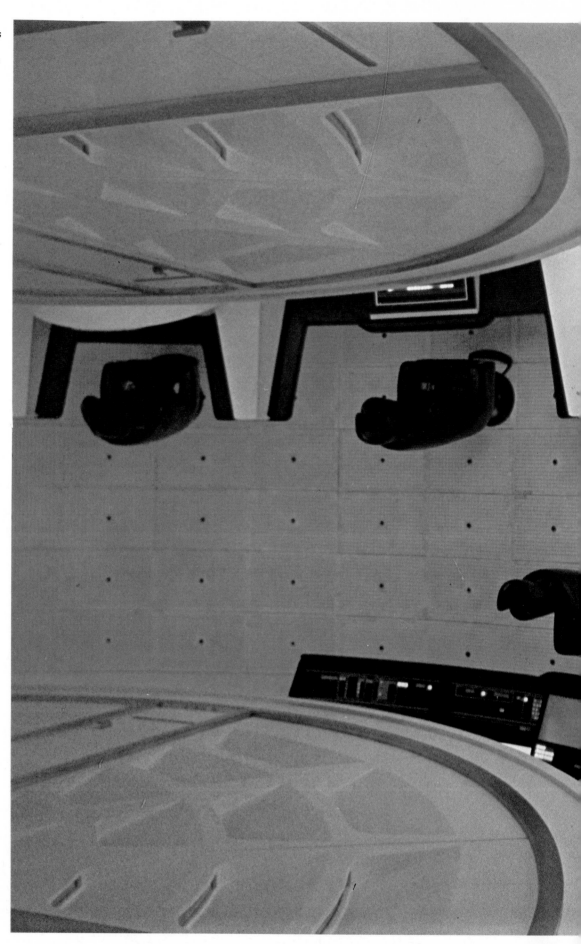

Exercise time on a space ship. Gary Lockwood takes his morning warm-up in 2001: A Space Odyssey.

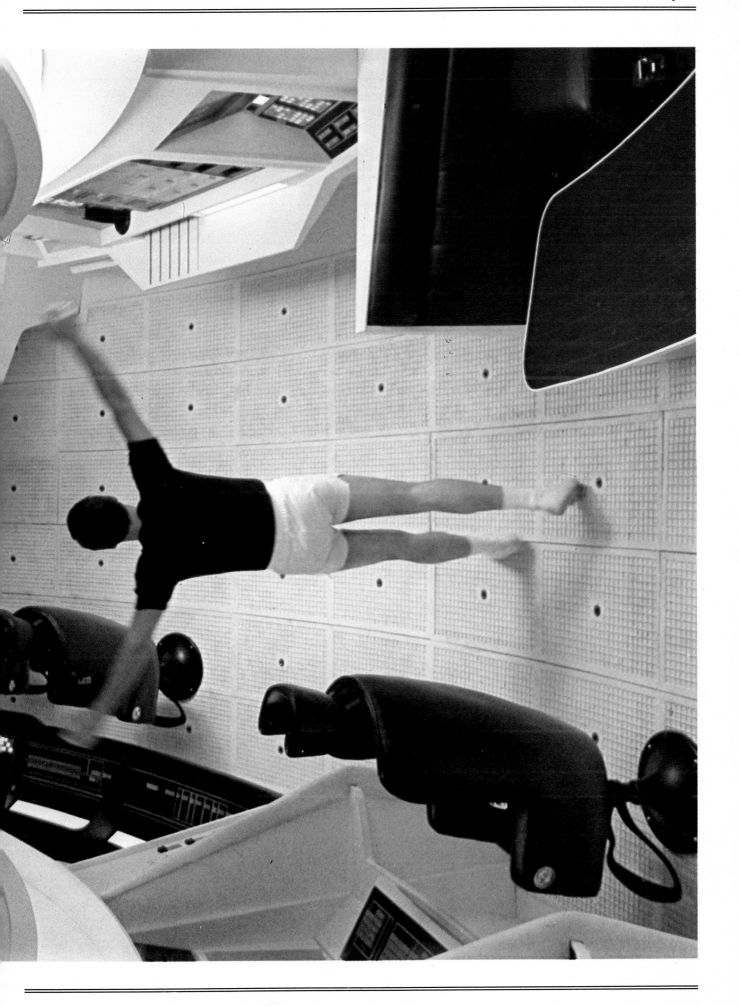

Opposite, top: *Keir Dullea, right, and Gary Lockwood in 2001: A Space Odyssey. They are trying to get out of range of Hal, the malign computer.*
Bottom: *Journey's end? Keir Dullea arrives on Jupiter, and finds a disconcerting décor on that planet.*

screenplay, with Arthur C. Clarke, from the latter's short story *The Sentinel*, and his credit for the special photographic effects – 'designed and directed by' – only hints at his innovatory work (including front-projection, which quickly became commonly used). The film was photographed in Super Panavision and benefited enormously by being shown in Cinerama (the later one-projector system) in major cities.

It begins with 'The Dawn of Man'. Prehistoric man, struggling to survive, wakes one morning to find in his midst a black monolith. Its mysterious arrival prompts these creatures to examine a jaw-bone, and it is tossed in the air to become, after a quick fade, a space-ship – man's toy or man's weapon. For during that fade four million years have passed. When, later, a similar black column is excavated from the surface of the moon we may suppose interplanetary intervention in prompting man to see the possibilities of the jaw-bone as a tool – or a weapon. For the moment, however, Dr Floyd (William Sylvester) has not reached the moon: he meets some Russians, disturbed at something happening up there. The film dallies with gadgetry, of which the most taking is 'Voice Print', a machine replacing intergalactic customs officers. There is also an astral conference of obscure meaning, though as much a part of the pattern as the Dodo's tears in *Alice in Wonderland*. The discovery of the black slab in its crater is accompanied by another, that it is emitting signals in the direction of Jupiter – and it is at this point that the odyssey of the title begins, as two astronauts embark on the voyage to Jupiter.

They are Bowman (Keir Dullea) and Poole (Gary Lockwood), accompanied by three colleagues in suspended animation and an increasingly sinister computer, HAL-9000. The film's subtitle might be 'My Travels with a Recalcitrant Computer', for there develops a life-or-death struggle between the machine and Bowman. HAL, controlling the spacecraft, is childishly determined to show that it is in charge. It cuts off the life-support systems of the three sleeping astronauts and causes a mechanism to fail, so that Poole must move outside in his space-pod. Bowman is forced into a rescue operation, but loses Poole, while miraculously saving himself. He takes a screwdriver to HAL, and continues alone, to see the black slab again, whirling in space, as he is sucked into another dimension, beyond Jupiter. The ten minutes that follow, called for quick reference 'the psychedelic trip', are among the most hallucinating and exciting in all cinema, as we – replacing Bowman – are hurtled through an infinity of shapes and visions, representing, perhaps, the creation of the universe through all time. There is no space or time or, rather, there is a time-warp, for the aged and dying Bowman finds himself in a room which might, or might not be, of the 18th century. As Bowman reaches out for yet another monolith he becomes a foetus – of either an alien or another space-age man, depending on your interpretation.

The ending of this seminal movie is one of its least satisfactory features – and, according to Michael Moorcock was only reached after numerous others had been rejected. It is doubtful whether all other aspects of the film were under-

stood by all spectators. Few of the reviews were overwhelmingly favourable: 'Morally pretentious, intellectually obscure and inordinately long' said Arthur Schlesinger Jr, but 'intensely exciting visually, with that peculiar artistic power which comes from obsession . . . a film out of control, an infuriating combination of exactitude on small points and incoherence on large ones.' Many critics felt that Kubrick should be taken to task for the film's pretensions and the undoubted obscurities. For the same reasons the industry disliked the film – film people didn't understand it, because there had never been a film like it before. But audiences loved it, riveted from the opening sequence, set to Richard Strauss's *Thus Spake Zarathustra*, through the sequences of spacecraft moving through the galaxy, set to waltzes by Johann Strauss, to the 'head trip'. It was premiered in June 1968, six months before Apollo 8 took off for its trip round the moon. The Russians had been the first in space but it is probable that for most people – those, anyway, in the Western democracies – the Space Age really began in December 1968. For one thing, Apollo 8 transmitted pictures back to earth which were probably watched – during the Christmas period – by everyone with a television set. *2001* or, anyway, parts of it, was no longer a fantasy.

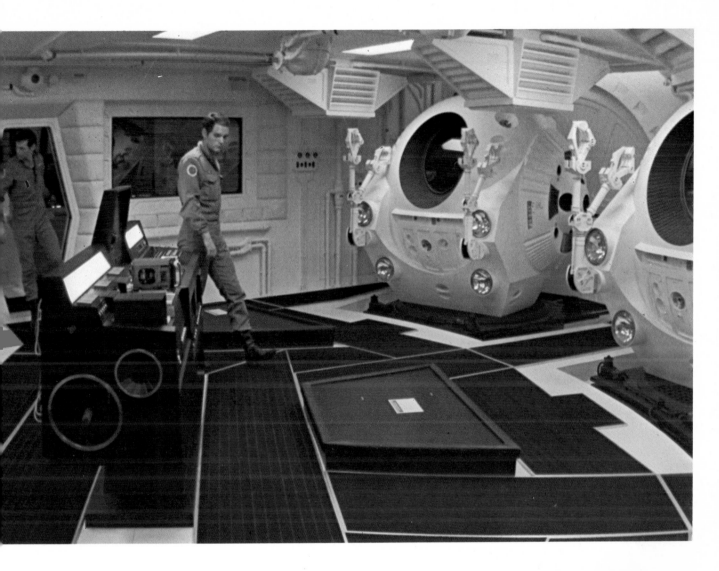

CHAPTER 5
In and Out of This World

The launching pad in The Man Who Fell to Earth. It
is from this that David Bowie hopes to embark on the
rescue of his family from his own – dying – planet.

Rod Steiger, in the title-role of The Illustrated Man. *You may not care for this picture of his back, but you may wonder how long it took the make-up department to paint these tatoos every morning of shooting.*

Below: *There is an untattooed patch on Mr Steiger's extensive anatomy and the drifter (Robert Drivas) realizes what it signifies for him. He accordingly prepares to cheat fate/tattooes if he can.*

THE film industry came round to admiring *2001*, as it continued to break records, but it was regarded as a freak success, especially when virtually every science-fiction movie that followed in its wake did not attract a wide public. The most promising was *The Illustrated Man* (1969), if only because for twenty years film-makers had been wanting to film Ray Bradbury's stories but could not get studio approval. The movie follows the format of the book, beginning with the seduction of an itinerant carnival worker, Carl (Rod Steiger), by a mysterious woman (Claire Bloom), who leaves him with his body covered in tattoos. As he searches later for the woman he falls in with a drifter who finds that when he 'reads' the tattoos they become narratives. In the first and best, *The Veldt*, two children are given a nursery which can be programmed to be any environment known to man, past or present. They choose the African veldt, to the exclusion of anywhere else, and when their parents object to the obsession they are lured inside, unable to find a way of getting to the mechanism as the unreal becomes frighteningly real. In *Long Rains*, four astronauts crash on Venus, where the perpetual torrent affects their beings and their minds as they try to reach the geodesic sundomes. *The Last Night of the World* is set as the world ends, in the 40th century. A government decree commands parents to murder their children to prevent them from suffering – but, alas,

this is not the first time a government has been wrong. When Carl's companion gazes into the only part of Carl's body which is not tattooed he can read the future and that reports back to him that Carl will kill him. Jack Smight, on other occasions an adroit director, proved to have too heavy a hand for this delicate material, and as much might be said for Mr Steiger, who with Miss Bloom appeared in all three stories as well as the framing device. His performances are distinctly over-mannered.

Steiger's almost universally bad reviews may have been one reason why audiences avoided this movie: it killed any further demand for science fiction fantasy, except for the Harryhausen pictures, to which I'll return later. In the meantime, there was, following *2001*, a dire warning to those who venture into space, as was explained by the very title *Marooned* (1969), which moved between the trapped astronauts, their anxious wives and those mounting the rescue operation. John Sturges, a notable action director, seems to have thought that the public would be interested in the meticulous technical details conveyed by the dialogue. It wasn't, despite the presence of such names as Gregory Peck (as the mission controller), Richard Crenna, David Janssen, James Franciscus and Gene Hackman.

Science-fiction was by now too firmly entrenched in cinemagoers' minds for it to die as the result of these two failures. But, it seemed, whenever film-makers' thoughts turned to the future they thought of Dystopia, probably because evil had always been better box-office than goodness. There was, of course, the happy example (in financial terms) of *Planet of the Apes*, where spectators had gladly paid to see a pessimistic vision of the future. That film, however, had had action adventure in the tradition of *The Time Machine*, to go no farther back. The visions of the future which now appeared were all determinedly grim. *No Blade of Grass* (1970) is another piece described by its title: industrial pollution has done its ecological worst, resulting in a worldwide famine, with a consequent breakdown of law and order. One London family traverses a dangerous Britain to seek safety with a relative in the Lake District, in the process becoming as brutalized as those from whom they are fleeing. The film is considerably inferior to its source, John Christopher's novel *The Death of Grass*, not helped by the over-emphatic direction of Cornel Wilde. Curiously, another former actor, Ray Milland, had directed (and in his case starred in) a similar tale, *Panic in Year Zero* in 1962, but in that tale the survival of the fittest was being tested after a nuclear war.

In *The Omega Man* (1971) a Sino-Russian germ war has killed off most of the world population. This story had been seen on screen before, as *The Last Man on Earth*, an Italian-American co-produc-

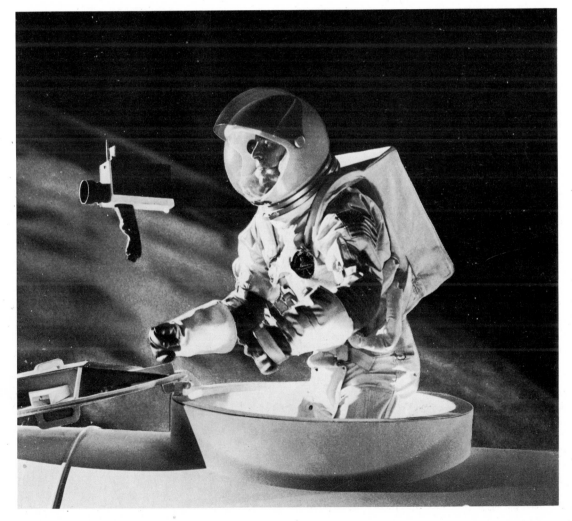

Marooned is the name of the movie and marooned is the problem, with three astronauts stuck within the orbit of the Earth, while Down Below a mission — in the face of an unkind Providence which complicates matters by sending a hurricane — prepares to rescue them. This is one of the unfortunates, James Franciscus.

The future, for the first prophets intent on looking at it, was going to consist of an inpersonal world where mankind had become, if not redundant, subservient to machines or theories. Later pundits, inspired perhaps by the inevitable breakdown which would follow a nuclear war – in the unlikely event of there being any survivors – foresaw civilization giving way to marauding bands. As here, in No Blade of Grass.

tion of 1964, in which Vincent Price played the sole survivor of a plague which has wiped out the world's population, except those existing as vampires. By night, he cowers in his apartment, playing records to drown out their cries. By day, he wanders about the streets with hammer and a stake to destroy any that he finds sleeping. The screenwriters of *The Omega Man* have replaced hammer and stake with a machine gun. They have reset the tale in Los Angeles in 1977 and added a number of banal comments on world peace. Charlton Heston now plays the last man on earth – only he isn't, since a religious fanatic, glimpsed on television, is in control of the 'Family' of vampires. When they come for Heston, he is woefully unfunny saying 'Tell me, are you fellows from the Internal Revenue Service?' But you may laugh as he says to a black seductress (Rosalind Cash), 'Kiddo, it has been a long, long time. I'm not certain how it goes,' to which she replies 'Are you ready for this? Birth control pills?' In the meantime we have had this dialogue. The girl's Dutch companion: 'You mean. . . ?' Heston: 'Yes, I'm immune. I could use my blood as serum.' Girl: 'You could save the world.' Boris Sagal's direction is no better than the dialogue, though there are some eerie sequences of Heston searching among long-dead corpses at desks or at dinner tables where they succumbed. But deserving much better is Richard Matheson's 1954 novel, *I Am Legend*, which is much more interesting than either of these film versions indicates.

THX 1138 (1971), directed and written from his own story by George Lucas (with an assist on the screenplay by Larry Murch), is preceded by some

scenes from a Buck Rogers serial, in the hope of reminding us how far the genre has advanced. This movie, on the other hand, is a very serious business, featuring a Dystopia more threatening and formidable than any hitherto encountered. Its inhabitants, known only by numbers, live in a computerized subterranean city guarded by metal-faced robots, their movements monitored by unseen cameras, their ears immune to electronic sounds – interrupted by chivvying speeches and news of disasters spoken by the sort of voices used by the similar systems in American department stores. THX 1138 (Robert Duvall) remains a cipher, perhaps by necessity; perhaps it was equally essential for the film to be completely humorless; but it fails not for these reasons but because we seem to have seen it all before – though never done with less tension.

Warner Bros, who distributed, loathed it, and the public avoided it, but in view of the director's later eminence a word of explanation is needed. George Lucas (b. 1944) left film school and became administrative assistant to the writer-director Francis Ford Coppola on *Finian's Rainbow*, during the making of which he decided – encouraged by the interest of the veteran writer-producer Carl Foreman – to turn his student movie, *THX 1138: 4EB* (winner of the National Student Film Award), into a commercial feature. Coppola stepped in, and *TXH 1138* became one of the batch of films which his company, American Zoetrope, was to make for Warner Bros, who purchased an option on the screenplay. Warner executives had seen the student version, and after examining the graphics designed by Lucas for the new one they sanctioned a budget of $777,777.77 (seven was Lucas's lucky number). This was a small budget by prevailing standards, but Warners' president, Ted Ashley, so despaired of seeing any of it returned that the deal with American Zoetrope was cancelled. In fact, he was so angry that he examined the $3.5 million paid to American Zoetrope for the development of scripts (paid after Coppola had finished making *The Rain People*), demanding that all material be turned over to Warners, plus a cash refund of $300,000. It was the sort of anger which did not allow for that customary movie practice, the write-off.

Lucas was bitter, though under no illusions about Coppola's plans for Zoetrope: 'Francis hoped to get a lot of young talent for nothing, make movies, and hope one of them would be a hit, and eventually build a studio that way.' One of the Lucas ideas peddled to Warners was a film on the Vietnam war – and that idea germinated in *Apocalypse Now*, which Coppola directed. But now, after the débâcle of *THX 1138*, Lucas was anxious to prove to the industry that he could make movies of wide appeal. Two concepts were advanced above the others: one was about teenagers in the early '60s, to be called *American Graffiti*, which was discussed by United Artists before Universal offered Lucas a mere $50,000 to write and direct, on a budget inferior to that for *THX 1138*. The other was a space age fantasy based on Flash Gordon and Buck Rogers. That became *Star Wars*.

There would be no place for Flash, Buck or even THX 1138 in *A Clockwork Orange* (1971), since it is set in a recognizable Britain. Warners produced, with results that compensated for the losses on *THX 1138* – financially, that is, for there is a debate as to its merits. The critics everywhere were enthusiastic, as if compensating for the luke-warm reception given to Stanley Kubrick's previous film, *2001*. Among those who found them suspect, apparently, was the editor of *The New York Times*, for when his critic Vincent Canby published his second rave notice there was printed alongside it the opposing view, by Clayton Riley, describing the film as 'a monumental bore'. After stating that I had inordinately admired all Kubrick's work for the cinema to that time, I have to say that I concur, though I would not use the word 'monumental' for something that seems to me essentially unimportant. I have to admit that I remain – all these years later – bewildered by my reaction: perhaps my expectations of Kubrick – especially after those reviews – were too high. I expected something daring, but found only a movie of modish violence, tiresome symbolism and with a muted but equally obvious message.

In Kubrick's future Britain (his screenplay was based on Anthony Burgess's novel), the government seems likely to be taken over by fascists. The apathetic population is terrorized by teenage hooligans, whose natural habitat seems to be milk-bars and the litter-strewn alleys of high-rise apartment blocks. Everyone is sex-obsessed: penises have been chalked on a huge mural of men in bathing-trunks; a woman is murdered with the giant china phallus she had as an objet d'art; bedroom walls are covered with nudes. The protagonist, Alex deLarge (Malcolm McDowell)

and his fellow droogs wear inflated jock-straps over their suits. They like a nice spot of rape or a threesome (in a jerked-up sequence which, as Mr Riley rightly said, is both amateurish and pointless). After raping one woman (Adrienne Corri) before her husband, an eminent writer, Mr Alexander (Patrick Magee), Alex traps another woman (Miriam Karlin) and murders her. Sent away to prison for fourteen years he submits, after an interview with the Minister whose idea it is, to the new right-wing government's project in reducing crime, by being brainwashed. He is pumped with drugs as films of pornography and violence are screened for him – and since their accompaniment is Beethoven's 9th Symphony his earlier passion for 'Ludwig van' has now become an abhorrence which also induces headaches and nausea. Alex returns to society ever prepared to turn the other cheek. His parents, however, have taken a lodger (Clive Francis) who has replaced him not only in his home but also in their affections. His old chums have become cops and have an old score to settle with him. They administer a brutal beating after which, in a pain-wracked stupor, he

A glimpse of the sterile world of THX 1138, *which starred Robert Duvall. The future, as conceived by George Lucas, who wrote and directed, offers a bleak prospect to most of us.*

Right: *Malcolm McDowell and his gang in* A Clockwork Orange. **Below:** *The gang on the rampage. Their victim is Adrienne Corri.* **Opposite:** *Alex (Malcolm McDowell) undergoing aversion therapy, designed to make him a more tractable member of society.*

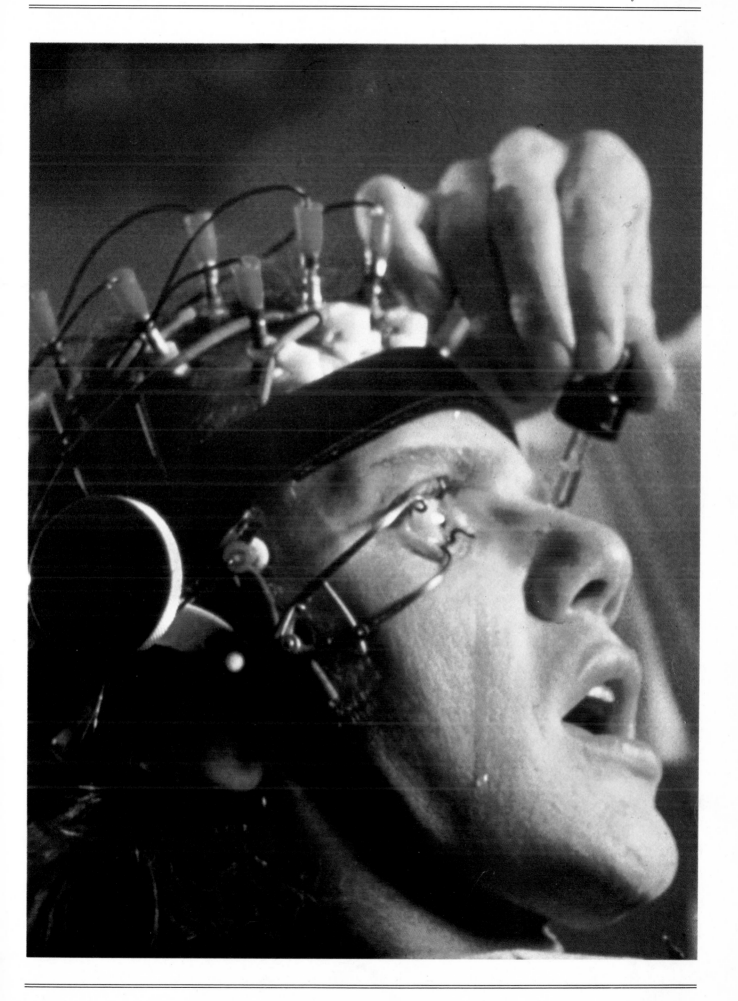

staggers to the door of the first house he sees and collapses on the threshold. He is taken in and succoured – by the writer, Alexander, a cripple now after the treatment to which Alec and his gang subjected him. Alexander recognizes him but Alec has no memory of Alexander; someone from his former existence, just another victim. He tells Alexander all that befell him and this is carefully recorded. Then Alexander imprisons Alec in a top-storey room and proceeds to drive him insane with an endlessly repeated tape, played fortissimo, of 'Ludwig van's' Ninth Symphony. To escape it, Alec crashes through the window; he is borne, broken and unconscious, to a hospital while Alexander (we later learn) pursues his plans to overthrow the government. When Alec, imprisoned in plaster and unable to feed himself, regains consciousness he has a surprise visitor – the Minister (Anthony Sharp). Alexander's conspiracy has been overthrown, and Alec begins to perceive the possibilities of his new rôle as a heroic survivor. In short, he is himself again – the drugs are out of his system now. The Minister is so willing to enroll him that he even feeds him, and the film ends with Alec embarking on bright prospects, supported by the government and accompanied by the strains of Ludwig van.

In *The New York Times*, Mr Riley put it thus: 'In extending the Burgess novel's thematic design to the screen, Kubrick has emphasized the book's notion that, in the name of free will, all self-expression becomes highly valued, even to the freedom to commit atrocities. That is, the will to perpetrate evil is better than no will at all.' In his book *The Science Fiction and Fantasy Film Handbook* Alan Frank writes 'Had the movie been the work of a lesser film maker, it is unlikely that it would have had the reception it received; as it is, his brutalization of Burgess' book has been taken for art rather than for its very strong exploitative elements which savour of a gloating admiration for the very violence it professes to deprecate.' Kubrick, who lives in Britain, controls the rights in that country and refuses to allow the film to be shown there again, reputedly on the grounds that British society has come much closer to that depicted in the film than would have been supposed when it was made. Ironically, Burgess's novel was inspired by the fact that his wife was raped by American soldiers in Britain during World War Two.

According to *Soylent Green* (1973), New York in 2022 AD will also be an unpleasant place. It is dirty, shabby, dangerous – New York as ever was – but shrouded in perpetual smog, enduring a permanent heatwave. Food is so short that the population has become derelict, crowded into empty churches where they are fed by charity and dressed in drab colours. Even our hero, a New York cop called Thorn (Charlton Heston) wears a nondescript shirt, joggers' pants and sneakers. He rooms with Sol (Edward G. Robinson), his 'book' or researcher, for learning is now confined to old fogeys buried among decaying files and library shelves. Thorn is assigned to investigate the murder of one of the few remaining rich men; what Sol learns about the case so distresses him that he checks into a clinic to die, aided by an injection, taped music and CinemaScope views of flowers. Thorn discovers the connection between the morgue and the new wonder food Soylent Green, a tablet much advertized on television. The blending of thriller elements – murder, corruption in high places – with this downbeat view of the future is hardly satisfactory, partly because the corruption is so pervading that audiences cannot care. Stanley R. Greenberg wrote the screenplay from a novel by Harry Harrison, *Make Room! Make Room!*, and it is also indebted to Pohl and Kornbluth's novel *The Space Merchants*, published twenty years earlier. In turn there would be elements of this film in *Coma* (the escape in the garbage truck) and *Death Watch* (the communities living in churches).

Set thirty-seven years later, the countryside of *Zardoz* (1974) makes the city of *Soylent Green* seem positively cosy. Scratching a meagre living from the acres of polluted wasteland are the Brutals, who have devised an armed master tribe to keep themselves in check, the Exterminators, who worship and are ruled by a giant godhead called Zardoz. One of their number, Zed (Sean Connery), stows away inside Zardoz and its cargo of grain, destined for the Vortex, the protected home of an élite called the Eternals. Inside the Vortex, a stately home with plastic domes, the Eternals dominate two more sub-tribes, the Renegades, some decrepit old people, and the Apathetics, who are zombies. The chief Eternals are sexless women who control the Exterminators by virtue of controlling Zardoz. Zed's action in arriving amongst them is a challenge to their power, and he is subjected to study by Consuella (Charlotte Rampling) and May (Sara Kestelman). Since they know not sexual desire they show him moving pictures of a woman fondling her breasts and two ladies mud-wrestling, to see whether these sexually excite him. They call him the Monster, asking him questions about his past and the world he had left behind. His past is shown on vast screens – and we learn that in some past life Zed stumbled on a library, and discovered that Zardoz was taken from 'The Wizard of Oz' – since the man behind the godhead is a practical joker. An occasional note of humour helps in a movie as incoherent as it is pretentious; no more than in *The Last Man on Earth* has the writer-director, John Boorman, produced either suitable or likely costumes for the future though his visual vitality is as potent as in his other films. It was said that he had wanted to film *The Lord of the Rings*: frustrated in his attempt to do that he has tried to come up with his own mythology, wrested from Tolkein, Bradbury and others.

Rollerball (1975) paints an equally gloomy picture of an earlier time, 2018, when the world has abolished warfare and eliminated both poverty and illness. Populations work off their aggression against each other by a game that combines elements of football, roller derby, hockey and motorcycle racing. After playing against Madrid, Houston's star player, Jonathan E (James Caan), finds himself requested to retire by the team of executives which run the world. Resenting the fact that one executive had appropriated his wife – whose image he watches on his multi-screen Video – Jonathan E sets out to discover why 'they' no longer want him. A dotty computer expert

Zardoz — Se 57.72.
Model of Stone against (Blue-Backing)
Plate of Dicklow Hills.

Above: *There are some magnificent isolated moments in Zardoz, including the giant flying head, seen here in the designer's interpretation, which gives the film its title.*

Left: *Another future you may not care to contemplate – the one in* Soylent Green, *where human beings are of such little account that they resemble the workers in* Metropolis. *The grab is a weapon for controlling riots.*

Rollerball – *the deadly game which gives the film its title, as played between nations now that war has been eliminated. Aggression, in the 21st century, is contained by the official sponsorship of these murderous contests.*

(Ralph Richardson) who has, incidentally, mislaid the 13th century, cannot throw any light on the situation; the executives, represented by Bartholomew (John Houseman) threaten reprisals if Jonathan E is not compliant and warn him by mentally mutilating his best friend (John Beck). His wife returns to beg him to quit Rollerball, but we do not know whether she has been brainwashed by the state or genuinely fears for his life while he is playing. The game was created, says someone, to take the place of individual initiative. 'Game?' responds Bartholomew, 'This wasn't meant to be a game.' In other words, the world of Rollerball is yet another Dystopia, with Jonathan E as the sole non-executive inhabitant with a mind. The director, Norman Jewison, offers some visual parallels with Roman epics; the game itself is like some form of gladatorial contest, and this is also a declining civilization where an élite rules and all the rest are pawns. Jonathan E is the one who dares to question, who dares to be a Christian. Or: this is the world of the old West, where one lone stranger pits himself against the might of the cattle barons. Or: he is the foreign correspondent in alien territory. Since audiences could be expected to find these analogies, the film was expected to find the popularity which had eluded *Soylent Green* and *Zardoz*, and the violence of the game was expected to help. But as the public remained indifferent United Artists must have wished that they had retained the title *The Roller-*

ball Murders, a short story by William Harrison, who also wrote the screenplay.

However, the industry was much less sanguine about *The Man Who Fell to Earth* (1976), produced by British Lion on the then huge budget of £1¾ million, and one of the last productions of that company – a fact not unconnected with another, that Paramount reneged on its agreement to distribute in the US after seeing the finished result. It is sadly without humour as written by Paul Mayersberg, from a novel by Walter Tevis, but the concept is promising. An alien (David Bowie) arrives on earth – the wilds of New Mexico – and, having studied us from afar, is able to pass himself off as a human, Thomas Newton. His own planet is dying, and he wants to construct a spacecraft in which to fetch his wife and child, bringing them to safety. To that end he has brought several scientific devices unknown to man, and with the help of a patent attorney, Farnsworth (Buck Henry), he becomes a millionaire, at least on paper. But when he orders Farnsworth to convert his assets into cash, so that he can begin work on the spacecraft, Farnsworth sets in chain a series of events which will unmask Newton and lead to his inability to return home. That, at least, is what may be learnt from the synopsis, but the film itself is elliptical to the point of alienation. All information is curtailed, a fate that might better have been meted out to the seemingly interminable shots of Newton and his girl friend indulging in sex or

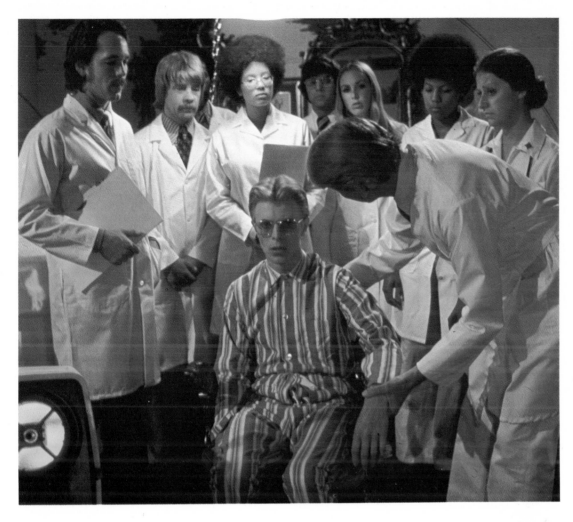

David Bowie in the title-role of The Man Who Fell to Earth. *Quite clearly, he has not long been here and those looks do not suggest someone with malevolent intentions.*

mooning around hotel rooms. The director, Nicolas Roeg, a former cameraman, is better at providing visual excitement than tension. Like Boorman with *Zardoz* he had attempted his own *2001* and failed.

On the other hand, there was hardly a warmer welcome for two better and much less pretentious genre movies, *The Andromeda Strain* (1971) and *The Terminal Man* (1974), both adapted from clever novels by Michael Crichton. Robert Wise directed the former, in which a satellite returns to earth with an alien virus capable of wiping out the earth's population – to judge it by its effect on the small Arizona town close to the landing point. In the laboratory complex constructed for just such emergencies a team of government scientists seek to destroy the virus while keeping surveillance on the town's two survivors, an aged drunk and a baby. Mike Hodges directed *The Terminal Man* (and also wrote the screenplay), which concerns one Harry Benson (George Segal), a paranoid psychotic who is afraid of machines. He also has an organic disease, and as he belongs to the medical profession he agrees, as an experiment, to have a computer installed inside his head. During the operation one doctor says 'You act like you're breaking into someone's tomb. It's only a head. Cut it,' so it's hardly surprising that when Harry comes round his zombie-like behaviour gives cause for alarm. Despite impressive visuals in both cases, the two films deteriorate; Crichton,

in his novels, was more able to keep at bay the B-picture elements. But *The Terminal Man* remains visually elegant, even when its horrors are much too reminiscent of *Psycho*.

Crichton himself became a film director with the ingenious *Westworld* (1973), which he also wrote. Westworld itself is one section of a theme park, Delos, where for $1,000 a day the visitor may indulge himself in the pleasures of the old West (or, in the other sections, Roman World or Medieval World). There to divert him are carefully-programmed human and animal-looking robots, whores to sleep with, gunslingers to be shot down. Could anything be more unknown than our secret desires and how they might be gratified? Such things used to happen in fairy tales and tales of the ancients, and thus *Westworld's* fantasy is linked to them. At the same time it shows what happens when the control room malfunctions and can no longer control the robots. For two Chicago business men (Richard Benjamin, James Brolin) their vacation becomes a nightmare after a black-garbed gunfighter (Yul Brynner), hitherto their quarry, does not behave as secret desires would wish. This is a film as witty as it is horrific and I think what makes it work is the contrast between the smug visitors, the falsely-smiling robots and the matter-of-fact technicians. It may have been inspired by *Deliverance*, in which the natural world exacts a severe price from some vacationers who have invaded it; in this case it is

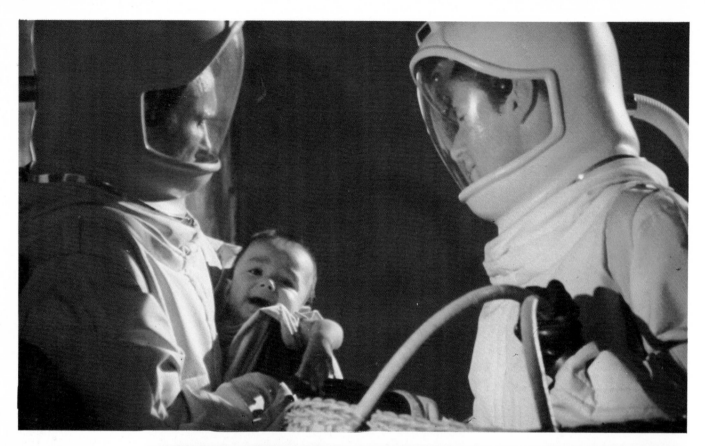

Above: *Many, many genre films concern a battle for survival – and the baby in* The Andromeda Strain *is one of two characters immune to a disease in a small Arizona town where everyone else has died. As such it is of great interest to the lab director (James Olsen), seen here with one of his assistants (George Mitchell).*

Right: *After a long interval that old staple of sci-fi, the creature being altered in a laboratory reappeared in 1974. In* The Terminal Man *it is a real operating theatre and a real man, played by George Segal; but when he emerges he behaves not unlike Frankenstein's monster.*

Opposite: *A robot in the theme park that is* Westworld. *This one looks like Yul Brynner, who indeed played the role.*

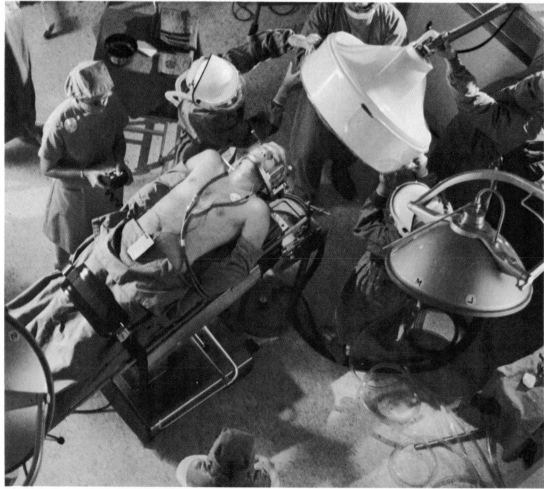

Bruce Dern in Silent Running, *one of the several movies of this period devoted to the premise that one sane man will survive against a world – or universe – gone mad. He is an astronaut confiding terrestrial vegetation to space in the hope that some will survive.*

the unnatural world which attacks.

Crichton had qualified as a doctor while making a name as a writer of thrillers and *Coma* (1978), which he directed and adapted – from Robin Cook's novel – shows him at home in a hospital. This one is in Boston, where a junior surgeon, Susan Wheeler (Genevieve Bujold), becomes disturbed by the number of patients leaving the operating table in a state of irreversible coma. The chief anaesthetist (Rip Torn) refuses to help, the chief surgeon (Richard Widmark) warns her to leave well alone and even her boy friend (Michael Douglas) behaves suspiciously. She eventually uncovers a vast international scheme whereby the bodies are put into suspended animation, to be sold, for large profits, for 'spare-part' surgery. *Coma*, like *Westworld*, is so well-sustained as a thriller that it is a shame that Crichton blundered on a more conventional tale, *The First Great Train Robbery*, set in Victorian England.

The actual business of space travel had not featured in these grim visions of the future, and that was probably because *Silent Running* (1972) had received as cool a welcome as *Marooned*. The director was Douglas Trumbull (b. 1943), a special effects expert whose *To the Moon and Beyond*, projected in 360-degree Cinerama, had been a feature of the 1964–5 New York World's Fair. Among those impressed had been Stanley Kubrick, who had hired Trumbull to work on *2001*. In the interim Trumbull had worked on *The Andromeda Strain*, but this film returned Trumbull to his speciality, of showing vast spacecraft seem-

ingly drifting towards the stars – and since it is set in 2001 we may suppose a homage to the earlier film. A spaceship is orbiting Saturn, with three astronauts who sit around playing cards; the other, Freeman Lowell (Bruce Dern), tends the plants and eats canteloupe melon. Scorned for dreaming, he retorts 'You don't think it's time someone had a dream again?' He resents an instruction on the intercom to 'abandon and nuclear-destruct all forests', of which there is a vast example up here. He decides to disobey orders and one of his companions is killed in the quarrel; the other two disappear, but he has as companion three androids till, after receiving a message that he's a good American, he is blown up. The obligatory downbeat ending surprises even less than usual on this occasion, for this concept goes nowwhere, clearly having nowhere to go. The screenplay by Deric Wasburn, 'Mike' Cimino and Steve Bocha is muddled, to put it kindly, but Trumbull's spacecraft remain beguiling to look at.

The First Men in the Moon (1964) are H. G. Wells's. The piece begins with a moon landing, anticipating the actual event by some years: there is found, disarmingly, a Union Jack and a note to the effect that the moon is claimed in the name of Her Imperial Majesty. A survivor of the expedition Arnold Bedford (Edward Judd), is found in Dymchurch, and the remainder of the film tells how he travelled to the moon, at the end of the 19th century, with his fiancée (Martha Hyer) and his neighbour Cavor (Lionel Jeffries), an eccentric

Very few science fiction movies are – or were – lighthearted, but The First Men in the Moon *is, as we may expect from its connection with Ray Harryhausen, whose movie fantasies never took themselves seriously. Notably good is Lionel Jeffries, as an elderly gentleman obsessed with the idea of reaching the moon. In the picture on the left he is making plans. It is obvious from the other picture, below, that he has arrived, accompanied by Edward Judd.*

engaged in scientific experiments. The tone of the film is set by Cavor's demonstration of his invention, a substance that defies the law of gravity, with Arnold floating to the ceiling in a chair. On the moon they have adventures of the usual sort, being separated and pursued by ant-like creatures, the Selenites, who live underground and are ruled by an indescribable creature which exists within what looks like a large green jelly. These were the invention of Ray Harryhausen, working as usual with the producer Charles H. Scheer. The director on this occasion was Nathan Juran, not quite matching the tongue-in-cheek performances of Judd and Jeffries, and the writers were *Quatermass*'s Nigel Kneale and Jan Read.

Harryhausen's other work at this time included the devising of prehistoric monsters for the 1966 Hammer remake of *One Million Years*, which was sillier than it needed to be, as directed by Don Chaffey with Raquel Welch, and for a 1969 Warner Bros action adventure, *The Valley of Gwangi*, directed by James O'Connelly with Richard Carlson and James Franciscus, in which said valley shelters said monsters, who are to be exhibited for modern eyes to feast upon. He was also responsible for the creature called *Trog* (1970), a man-ape in the care of anthropologist Joan Crawford (in her last film). Harryhausen's finest work, however, is in his versions of myths and legends: *Jason and the Argonauts* (1963), directed by Don Chaffey; *The Golden Voyage of Sinbad* (1973), directed by Gordon Hessler; *Sinbad and the Eye of the Tiger* (1977), directed by Sam Wanamaker; and his masterpiece, *Clash of the Titans*. Whether filming Swift (*The Three Voyages of Gulliver*), Verne (*Mysterious Island*), the Greeks or the Arabian Nights, Harryhausen is closer to comic strips than the originals. The acting is rudimentary, the dialogue pedestrian and the settings sometimes garish; but Harryhausen understood and loved the cinema's capacity for fantasy. He sent his

Ray Harryhausen's heroes set out on long, dangerous journeys, usually by sea, confront numerous hazards upon making landfall, and end with a deadly confrontation. In this scene from The Golden Voyage of Sinbad *the hero (John Phillip Law) meets small creatures – but that is no guarantee of safety. The film features another of Harryhausen's creatures, the magic talisman which accompanies Sinbad.*

heroes on perilous voyages, where strange creatures swam beneath the deep waters, to arrive in weird, inhospitable landscapes where even more dangerous monsters lurked; and there were often human enemies, sometimes equipped with magical powers. You may not be taken in by all Harryhausen's tricks, but the superior ones are such that they make us indulgent to those which work a little less well.

Compare them, for instance, to the series of films produced by John Dark and directed by Kevin Connor, *The Land That Time Forgot* (1974), *At the Earth's Core* (1976), *The People That Time Forgot* (1977) and *Warlords of Atlantis* (1978). The first three, based on novels by Edgar Rice Burroughs, were produced by Amicus for British Lion, with participation by American International on the third; the fourth was produced by EMI, probably because British Lion was defunct by that time. Starring in all four was a former television favourite, Doug McClure, who manages to be quite energetic, despite looking as though he had been having a heavy time of it the night before – and that is a considerable achievement, for the action is almost non-stop. And there, rather than in the plastic dinosaurs, lies the disability of these films. Given the dreadful dialogue, the one-dimensional characters and the variable special effects it might have seemed like a good idea to make the action continuous, but in practice the law of diminishing returns prevails. The plots are much of a muchness, whether set in the early

years of this century (as in the Burroughs films) or earlier (as in the last of them). Either by design or accident a group of explorers/scientists arrives in a strange territory where the fauna, if not the flora, has remained the same for several millenia.

Among the other creative people whose names appear among the credits of these films are Max J. Rosenberg and Milton Subotsky, executive producers and/or screenwriters of *Dr Who and the Daleks* (1965) and *Daleks – Invasion Earth 2150 AD* (1966), both directed by Gordon Flemying. Their importance lies in bringing to the cinema Dr Who, whose popularity over two decades had much to do with the wider acceptance of science-fiction. When Dr Who first appeared on BBC television in 1963, he was a simple time traveller and indeed in the very first episode he took visitors back to the Stone Age, the French Revolution and the gunfight at the O.K. Corral. It was soon established that Dr Who could also move forward in time, and the introduction of the Daleks – space age enemies in robot form – in 1964 widened the programme's popularity. From that time what had been a mediocre children's programme grew in sophistication, eventually attracting a wide audience of grown-ups also. The third of the five Dr Whos (or six, if we count Peter Cushing in the two cinema films) was Tom Baker, who took over in 1974, not long after playing Rasputin in the prestigious *Nicholas and Alexandra*. Partly on the strength of his name the BBC sold a package of the programmes to PBS (America's publicly-

Star Trek takes place in the 23rd century, when the alien, Mr Spock (Leonard Nimoy) of the planet Vulcan, helps the gallant Admiral Kirk (William Shatner) on the USS Enterprise. *They worked together in harmony in the television series, and since cinema patrons were to expect something more than two or three episodes strung together the movie went by the grand title* Star Trek – the Motion Picture. *The illustration opposite was the basis for the art work for the advertising. To the right of Mr Shatner, aficionados will recognise DeForrest Kelley as Doctor 'Bones'.*

funded network), but they failed to arouse much interest. After the success of *Star Wars* the BBC sold another package to the States for syndication, when the programme picked up a cult following.

Something similar happened with *Star Trek*, which began on NBC in 1966. In 1964 the film producer Irwin Allen had sold a series, *Voyage to the Bottom of the Sea*, based on his 1961 movie, to ABC. The following year he placed his *Lost in Space* series with CBS, which had briefly considered *Star Trek*, as conceived by a leading television writer, Gene Roddenberry, which he envisaged as a space age *Wagon Train*. Allen's two series were successful, and when ABC had its much bigger bonanza with *Batman* NBC felt it imperative to get into the space-age act. The more adult formula planned for *Star Trek* meant that it would be no mere copy. *Star Trek* was set aboard a giant space-craft, USS Enterprise, bound – two hundred years in the future – for the United Federation of Planets. Paramount, which had produced, put the series into syndication after it had succumbed to audience apathy during its third season, and *Star Trek* took on a new lease of life. An animated

version was televised in the early '70s, to be followed in 1979 by *Star Trek – the Motion Picture*, which to date has spawned two sequels for cinemas. But no matter how many Star Trekkies there were, nor how vociferous, the first of those three films was made because world audiences had endorsed one sci-fi movie as few others in the history of cinema.

That movie was *Star Wars* (1977), written and directed by George Lucas, whose *American Graffiti* had been a big success for Universal. That company, however, turned down the chance of producing *Star Wars* and Lucas took it to 20th Century-Fox, which assigned a budget of $9.5 million. That represented a risk, but *2001* had cost a million more than that, and after decent profits on its initial release had had several equally successful reissues. In charge of the special effects was a protégé of Douglas Trumbull's, John Dykstra, who benefited from the technical advances made since Kubrick's film: that had had only thirty-five separate composites and *Star Wars* had over ten times that number. Also, as Dykstra observed, Kubrick's spacecraft had been linear

The Allies confer in Star Wars. *From left to right: Chawbacca, C-3PO, R2-D2, Mark Hamill and Alec Guinness.*

while his could be seen from several angles – as they, in miniature, reversed or rotated before the camera, which was also able to move between them in its 75-feet trench.

To the few who may have recalled *THX 1138*, it would not have been surprising that the inspiration of *Star Wars* was provided by the Buck Rogers-Flash Gordon serials. The long written introduction, with the words disappearing into infinity, recalls Hollywood epics of a past age; whilst the actual plot is a reworking of elements in T. H. White's retelling of the Arthurian legends, *The Once and Future King*. Basically, the princess (Carrie Fisher) is captive in the enemy's castle, and our intrepid hero Luke Skywalker (Mark Hamill) sets out to rescue her, accompanied by a motley group of companions: that done, he leads her people to vanquish the enemy. The difference is that she's not in a castle but a space-station, but it has the equivalent of drawbridge and portcullis, just as a laser-beam is the equivalent of a sword. The head of the enemy is Peter Cushing; the companions in adversity are a mercenary/space captain (Harrison Ford), a sage/warrior knight (Alec Guiness), a huge animal, not unlike the Cowardly Lion of *The Wizard of Oz*, and a couple of robots called C-3PO and R2-D2.

These, and other examples of *Star Wars* hardware, were copied, to appear in toyshops the world over. The appeal of *Star Wars* to children cannot be underestimated, nor the use of merchandizing in the success of the sequels, *The Empire Strikes Back* (1980), directed by Irvin Kershner, and *The Return of the Jedi* (1983), directed by Richard Marquand. The reviews of the three films were in general good for the first one but poor for the other two. Taken into account the higher admission prices the initial release of *The Empire Strikes Back* would seem to have attracted approximately only sixty per cent of those who went to see *Star Wars*. At $193,500,000 domestic* *Star Wars* is the second highest grossing film yet made (after *E.T.: the Extra-Terrestrial*); at $141,600,000 *The Empire Strikes Back* is the fourth – but over $20 million of this came from two reissues, before and after the *Jedi* returned. At $165,500,000 *The Return of the Jedi* is the No 3 all-time box-office success. If a guide geared to inflation were used, these figures would be dwarfed by such earlier box-office successes as *Gone with the Wind* and *The Sound of Music*; but even if cinema prices have doubled between *Star Wars* and *The Return of the Jedi* this is still a remarkable achievement. When many much-touted contemporary films fail to take $2 million at the box-office, the two re-releases of *The Empire Strikes Back* must be regarded as a spectacular success. And, interestingly, this film is the most considered and mature of the three.

The popularity of *Star Wars* encouraged Lucas to spend over $32 million dollars on the two sequels, and the reported 545 special effects in the original had risen to 942 for *Jedi*, the majority provided by Industrial Light and Magic, a Lucasfilm subsidiary which was founded on the profits of the first film. In the six years between that and *Jedi* movie technology had been transformed. Lucas's dedication to his films and his

The American and Canadian figures, which the industry itself uses as a barometer of success for quick reference.

audiences can be measured by some of the marvellous effects, by the wizardry which has gone into the production of the films. Lucas himself wrote *Star Wars*, planned to be Part IV of a series of eight; Lawrence Kasdan worked on the other two, Parts V and VI with, in the first instance, Leigh Brackett, and in the second, Lucas. The selection of Miss Brackett was interesting, for she was a distinguished writer of thrillers and science-fiction as well as a contributor to the screenplays of several movies directed by Howard Hawks, including *The Big Sleep*. Between his two contributions Kasdan, already a screenwriter much in demand, had made an impressive directorial debut with *Body Heat*, but as he said himself Lucas wanted to get the best possible screenplay. Unfortunately the screenplays of both *Empire* and *Jedi* give the effect of having been cobbled together after the special effects were dreamed up. The stories are shapeless, built round battles with ray-guns and exploding machines. We may be glad that the parodies of many other movie genres, a major feature of *Star Wars*, have been dropped, but there is no compensating humour. Virtually the sole laugh in *Jedi* is when one machine gets its lead caught around a tree and is travelling at such momentum that it crashes into it – and even as we laugh we may care to bear in mind that Lucas himself went into a tree during adolescence.

Even as a grand design emerges in the three films, the relationship of Luke Skywalker with the faceless enemy warrior who is his father, Darth Vader, it is crippled by the fact that Luke, the Princess and Hans Solo have no more dimension than the robots and furries which make up the rest of the cast. (Neither Hamill nor Miss Fisher has had any other major movie success, and though Mr Ford unquestionably has he is not an action hero remotely of the quality of a Clark Gable or a Gary Cooper). When, at the end of *Jedi*, the Emperor tries to convert Luke to the 'dark side' of the Empire, he cannot; nor can he kill him by shooting into him more electric currents than were used in the entire catalogue of Frankenstein movies. Superman, as we shall see, will have an evil alter-ego, and he will be seriously incapacitated by his enemies. Here everything is what it is said to be, immutable; so while the Superman movies offer, albeit in their own way, the possibilities of humanity, the *Star Wars* trio offers only the impossibilities of the comic strip. When Luke burns his father on a funeral pyre, in the manner of the Vikings – that father who betrayed him, in the manner of the Greeks – we know that Lucas has read the classics. But he hasn't understood them. The Ancients wanted us to wonder at the diversity of thought and experience available to mankind; Lucas wants us to wonder at the diversity of thought and experience of creations who by their own definition have almost none.

As I write there are no plans to film the other projected five movies of the series, but doubtless the stockholders of 20th Century-Fox will be happy when they continue, as will the countless aficionados. Lucas may be hesitating, not wanting to tempt providence a fourth time. He may be content, for in this trilogy he created a phenomenon, even to an industry accustomed to phenomena.

From The Return of the
Jedi *the 'things' which
have endeared themselves
to audiences in all three
films.* **Left:** *Yoda, the sage
and* **above**, *the two
contrasting robots, C-3PO
(left) and R2-D2.*

CHAPTER 6

Fantasy and Science Fiction

If they come, will they look like this? The Unidentified Flying Objects of Close Encounters of the Third Kind, *seen by Melinda Dillon, left. UFOs was the description accorded to such looked-for phenomena in the 1950s.*

To the generation growing up with them the heroes of *Star Wars* were what the movie cowboys and swordsmen had been to earlier audiences. Indeed, after the failure of some Westerns and swashbucklers in the '60s and '70s the film industry had lost enthusiasm for these standbys of former times and had virtually ceased making them. With the success of *Star Wars* itself the industry turned to sci-fi with a vengeance: on the screen it began to change. It became, often, pure fantasy. The fantasies necessary to its existence had always had a dark hue; one reason that it had often been bracketed with horror stories was that both dealt to a great extent with the unknown. The writers of science-fiction – or since we are dealing with movies, the visualizing of it, perhaps we should say 'the creators' had often had deep forebodings about the future. Inter-planetary travel seemed inevitably to be accompanied by conflicts between man and machines, between man and aliens, between man and androids, between man and creatures, even, of his own imagination. Many, if not all, of the dire fates overtaking the earth were due to mankind's stupidity in playing with nuclear weaponry. Man was unable to control the forces let loose by the advances in scientific knowledge; he had, simply, a tiger by the tail.

The first science-fiction films of the '50s were predicated on the consequences of living in a nuclear age. One film of the '70s allied science-fiction to war – the 1939–45 war, and without reference to the two atom bombs which concluded

it. *Slaughterhouse-Five* (1972) was in fact one of the great failures of its time, but it was one of the few recent occasions that a genre movie has been based on a novel by a leading writer, in this case Kurt Vonnegut Jr. His hero, Billy Pilgrim – played in the film by Michael Sachs – is meant to be a twentieth-century Everyman. As the movie starts, he is a man of some standing in his community, in upstate New York. He is, significantly, an optometrist by profession, who now is troubling himself with the local paper, claiming that he has been 'unstuck in time' since his days as a prisoner of war, when he survived the bombing of Dresden. That autobiographical element (Vonnegut's novel was forged from his own nightmare memories) is handled in the film with sobriety; everything else in Billy's life – childhood, marriage, the present – is shown as grotesque, to indicate that all is fantasy except that horrible reality. After his wife's death Billy gives himself up entirely to his fantasies and is transported to the planet of Tralfamadore, where he lives in a glass dome sealed off from the cyanide air outside. He is given a companion in the luscious form of Montana Wildhack (Valerie Perrine), a Hollywood starlet whom he had admired as a Playboy centre-fold. Otherwise the inhabitants of Tralfamadore live in the fourth dimension – or so he is informed by a disembodied voice. The voice informs him that there are thirty-one inhabitants but only on earth is there free will. That statement is followed by a continuation of the shots of the bombing of Dresden, and that, of course, is the point of the film. The message, unfortunately, is muted. Although the director, George Roy Hill, and the screenwriter, Stephen Geller, have treated the German sequences – the title refers to the German prison camp where Billy is housed – with respect they have failed to find the correct tone for the rest of the film, which increasingly betrays Vonnegut's intentions.

Close Encounters of the Third Kind (1977) had something similar to say – eventually. It owed its inspiration directly to the films of warning of the early '50s, most notably *It Came From Outer Space*. The first kind of Close Encounter is the sighting of a Ufo and the second is proof of its physical existence; the third is contact with its entity and/ or occupants – and that, as promised, is where Steven Spielberg's film leads us, sometimes dopily but often thrillingly. His protagonist is a powerline repair worker, Roy Neary (Richard Dreyfuss), who becomes obsessed with the Ufos being sighted near his home in Indiana. His interest in the subject loses him his job; after sighting the Ufos he begins to be obsessive about a hill, finally grabbing garbage and half the garden to build one in his living room. Neighbours and wife think him mad, but it seems that one of the Ufos created a telepathic vision within his head, for his hill is a model of Devil's Tower in Wyoming where, it turns out, the American army has arranged to receive what may be the first friendly landing of a flying saucer. With a woman (Melinda Dillon) whose child has been stolen by the invisible presences he evades the army and other visionaries to spy on the landing, but is finally asked by the army to join their team of space volunteers. The aliens turn out to be the usual moon-men of sci-fi, but definitely

Michael Sachs in one of the prisoner of war camp flashback sequences of Slaughterhouse-Five. *An ambitious polemic, the film looks to the horror of the past as well as warning of the probable horrors of the future.*

wanting to be at peace with the earth – provided, that is, that the earth wants to be at peace with itself.

Other sources raided by Spielberg are the James Bond film, *You Only Live Once*, for the landing pad finale, and *Dr Strangelove*, for its attitude to the military (this film originally concluded with a song, 'When You Wish Upon a Star', in emulation of *Strangelove*'s 'We'll Meet Again', but it was deleted after the previews.) He has worked his way carefully to his quasi-religious message at the end, so that matters of inconvenience – hysteria or panic at the prospect of extra-terrestials landing – are either glossed over or ignored. But inconsistently these Ufos let loose terrifying invisible presences which wreck houses by turning on every available mechanical gadget, with great winds and light, yet they turn out to be not only benign but of superhuman intelligence. Spielberg himself loves gadgetry, and the film's climax is an astounding parade of incandescent, amorphous Ufos, which he designed with Douglas Trumbull. Columbia had had little hesitation on allocating the then-huge budget of $18 million, because of the success of *Jaws*, which Spielberg had made for

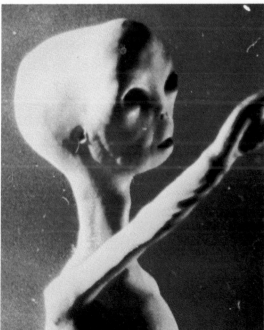

Above: *The starship moving into view over Devil's Mountain, Wyoming.*
Left: *One of those who travelled on the star ship and brought about* Close Encounters of the Third Kind.

Two worlds meet on our world. The starship prepares to leave, and a group of earthmen go with her. Close Encounters of the Third Kind.

Universal. But the studio became nervous as a series of flops meant that its future depended on *Close Encounters*. As it turned out it enjoyed a huge popularity, not unconnected with the fact that it followed *Star Wars* into cinemas. These were the two sides of science-fiction: *Star Wars* was fantasy and this was, or pretended to be, very much of our world. Most people decided that they had to see both, but it is doubtful whether any but the most credulous would find the message of *Close Encounters* any more impressive than the high jinks of *Star Wars*. In 1980 Spielberg issued *Close Encounters of the Third Kind: The Special Edition*, which had removed from the original 16 minutes of material but was only three minutes shorter, for some rejected material had been reinstated and some more filmed specially. The changes allowed for the trimming of that sequence in which Neary goes berserk in starting to build his mountain and more time to the deteriorating relationship with his wife. He also, now, is given a guided tour of the alien mothership.

The opening of *Superman* (1978) is more certifiably mumbo jumbo, as we are introduced to powers good and evil on the planet of Krypton, which is about to be destroyed. That, it seems, is why Superman's parents (Marlon Brando, Susannah York) decided to send him to earth in a time capsule. It arrives like a meteor in Arizona, where a childless couple (Glenn Ford, Phyllis Thaxter) adopt the small boy. Soon enough he's holding up a truck which might have injured his 'father'; as a teenager he can run faster than a train. After bidding his now-widowed 'mother' farewell he has a rendezvous with his father's spirit somewhere near the North Pole, to turn up some years later in New York – called in the Synopsis Metropolis – as a clumsy, bespectacled reporter in a three-piece suit called Clark Kent. He meets a colleague, Lois Lane (Margot Kidder), and faints when they are held up by a petty crook: what she doesn't know is that he had grabbed the crook's bullet, in flight. A few minutes later, Lois is in a helicopter which crashes into a skyscraper, from which she is dangling. Clark Kent finds her bag in the street; with a determined grin he pulls away his shirt to reveal the large S which denotes his name. As he soars to the skies so does the film, and thereafter it can do no wrong.

Superman's enemy is Lex Luthor (Gene Hackman), who lives with his cohorts, the idiotic Otis (Ned Beatty) and the glamorous Miss Teschmacher (Valerie Perrine) in a flat below Grand Central station. Luthor, of course, plans to dominate the world, and to make himself wealthy he is buying up real estate in California which will double in value after he has sent a rocket through the Saint Andreas Fault to cause the coastal area to fall into the sea. He also gets Superman in his power for a while, by flinging at him a piece of kryptonite, stolen from a museum in Addis Ababa, but Superman is released by Miss Teschmacher after Luthor has interfered with a couple of rockets, one of which is bound for Hackensack, where her mother lives. Superman flies not only in the sky but through the flames of the Fault. Towards the end the special effects, mostly superb, become a little ragged, and it was perhaps a mistake to un-earth, as it were, the earthquake

which had presumably killed Lois. In the strip-cartoon original Superman was never allowed to interfere with history, and even a jokey film like this should not betray our knowledge of the feasible, for we might even doubt that we are watching Superman fly. The flying scenes provide enchantment, and that in which Superman takes Lois over the Statue of Liberty cleverly indicates to adult viewers – and precocious children – that it's an allegory for a prolonged orgasm. Elsewhere the film is true to the tenets of the comic-strip, at its most disarming as Superman modestly acknowledges the cheers of the populace. Its Superman/Clark Kent is Christopher Reeve, who is virtually faultless; if Superman requires only his looks and his brawn his bumbling reporter is increasingly likeable.

The guiding force behind the film was Pierre Spengler, who had worked with the father and son team of producers Alexander and Ilya Salkind on the 1973 version of *The Three Musketeers*. That became two films after it was discovered that sufficient material had been shot. Some of the material filmed for *Superman* was similarly incorporated by the Salkinds into *Superman II* (1980), but then the production of both films was fraught with difficulty. It took a long while, despite the failure of *Batman*, to negotiate the rights with D. C. Comics; for a long while the backers insisted upon Robert Redford for the lead, but he did not like the script (finally credited to Mario Puzo, David Newman, Leslie Newman and Robert Benton, from a story by Puzo). Brando expressed interest in a role and there was worked out an extraordinary fee of what was said to be $3½ million for twelve days' work – and then he refused to work in Italy, so production was shifted to Britain. The director, Guy Hamilton, was replaced by Richard Donner, fresh from *The Omen*. At one point *Superman* looked permanently stalled, since so many writs were flying about London. Warners presumably came to the rescue to protect their investment, and although we were assured that from 40 to 60 per cent of *Superman II* existed as the first film premiered it did not go into production till much later, and then after many difficulties and much recrimination among some of the parties involved. The $25 million cost of the first film had been amply justified by the box-office reception, so there was little point in rehiring Brando for prestige or any other reason. Richard Lester, who had directed *The Three Musketeers* and had advised on *Superman*, replaced Donner. David and Leslie Newman wrote *Superman II* from a story by Puzo, and this husband and wife team are the only survivors of the original four to have worked on *Superman III* (1983), also directed by Donner. Despite the distinction of all these names (David Newman and Benton had made their reputations with *Bonnie and Clyde*) we might suppose the three Superman films to have been made by committee; but all three show a mastery of the space-age fantasy film which I do not think has been equalled elsewhere.

Superman II has more humour than *Superman*, and it lacks the portentousness of the earlier film's opening. It gets Superman flying in the first reel, to dislodge an H-Bomb from the Eiffel Tower – where Lois has been caught underneath the lift,

going up and down like a yo-yo. The sequence has an energy which may make us forgive for once the use of nuclear warfare as merely a facet of boys' adventure. Superman hurls the lift into outer space – where the explosion releases from the fragment of kryptonite in which they have been one-dimensionally imprisoned General Zod (Terence Stamp) and his evil partners, Ursa (Sarah Douglas) and Non (Jack O'Halloran). These arrive in the US, wreaking a trail of destruction – something to which they themselves are impervious. Uncertain what to do in this land of mortals, Zod learns that the US president (E. G. Marshall) is the mightiest of them and in effect the world leader. Zod determines to make him bow to him, at which point Lex Luthor (Hackman) arrives,

hoping to ally himself with Zod by leading him to Superman – who at that point is planning to become human so that he can marry Lois.

Superman III, in Lester's own word, is more 'earthbound' – partly because of the presence of Richard Pryor; and partly because of him it is even funnier. Pryor plays an out-of-work schmuck who becomes, by chance, the world's leading computer expert, able to swindle his boss (Robert Vaughan) out of millions. Said tycoon decides to use Pryor's skills to ruin Colombia's coffee crop – and although that scheme is foiled by Superman, Pryor is required to do for oil what he tried to do to coffee, thereby ensuring that his boss owns the world's supply and will thus become its master – the world's, that is.

One of the most cheering spectacles the cinema has to offer – Superman in flight. He, played by Christopher Reeve, is seen in Superman – The Movie, *to give its correct title.*

Right: *Superman in the ice caves, carrying a multitude of secrets in his hand.*

Opposite, top: *Marlon Brando, at the right in the picture, played Reeve's father in the first of the three films, and he is seen here with the three super criminals of Krypton, Ursa (Sarah Douglas), Non (Jack O'Halloran) and General Zod (Terence Stamp), who would turn up in the second film to so mightily challenge Superman's strength and imagination.*

Bottom: *Superman III was equally a vehicle for the comic, Richard Pryor, playing the world's greatest computer expert. Here is the world's greatest computer challenging him.*

Opposite: *The planet Mongo, as designed by Danilo Donati for* Flash Gordon.

Right: *Zarkov's space ship makes heavy landfall. The craft which takes Flash, Dale and Zarkov to Mongo.*

Below: *The court of Ming the Merciless (Max von Sydow), who can be seen standing at the top of the steps with his high priest, Klytus, played behind a mask by Peter Wyngarde. In front of Klytus is Prince Barin (Timothy Dalton).*

Our cloaked hero flies less in *Superman III*, for the people who made these films are canny: they never give us enough of a good thing. The duels, magnificent and scarey in *Superman II*, may be a little less effective, but they include one between Clark Kent and an evil Superman, to show that this hero is not always god-like. Lester's input of 'reality in all this nonsense' may be one reason why the third Superman film is a mite less splendidly enjoyable than the others. But the trio as a whole is a triumph of movie technology.

Superman's success meant the resuscitation of *Flash Gordon* (1980), expensively produced by Dino de Laurentiis, with direction by Michael Hodges and a screenplay by Lorenzo Semple Jr who had written the 1966 Batman. He had since done much better tongue-in-cheek work on this producer's excellent remake of *King Kong*. But this Flash Gordon only limps along in the shadow of Superman. The sophisticated talents involved have had the same difficulties, of turning a minor diversion, a comic strip, into the sort of movie millions will love – with parody, spectacle, a more complex plot than the original (to hold the adults in the audience) and affection. On the last count *Flash Gordon* is completely deficient. In the title-role, Sam J. Jones has to play on one note throughout. A great actor, Max Von Sydow, is made a 'campy' villain, but one not to be compared with Boris Karloff in *The Mask of Fu Manchu*. From that film comes the lascivious daughter (Ornella Muti), who so lusts after Flash that when he is revived from the dead her lover (Timothy Dalton) accuses her of adding necrophilia to her other interests. The range of sexual activity up there on Mongo seems to be considerable, but no more than *Barbarella* (an earlier effort

of this producer) is the film erotic. The exposition is in traditional form, as Flash and an air hostess, Dale Arden (Melody Anderson), crash into the laboratory of Dr Hans Zarkov (Topol), who has the theory that the moon will crash into the earth, having been diverted from its usual axis by evil forces in the universe. He kidnaps the couple and within minutes they are on Mongo and in the power of Ming the Merciless. After that the non-stop action is complicated without being complex, while the climax has more battles with ray-guns than in all three *Star Wars* movies, plus, for the record, Flying Monkeys borrowed from *The Wizard of Oz*.

Christopher Reeve himself appeared in an interesting variation on the theme of time travel, *Somewhere in Time* (1980), directed by Jeannot Swarc and adapted by Richard Matheson from his novel, *Bid Time Return*. Reeve plays a modern dramatist who recognizes in a hotel's 'Hall of History' an Edwardian beauty who, as an old lady, once gave him a watch and whispered 'Come back to me.' He learns more about her, about time travel, and the fact that she stayed at the hotel in 1912. Buying the appropriate duds, he wills himself back in time, but alas to a plot which, when not thin, is too reminiscent of such films of the '30s as *Peter Ibbetson* and *Maytime*. In fact, the film sets out to appeal to the romantically-minded but it is not sufficiently full-blooded.

More successful both as romance and science fiction is *Death Watch/La Mort en Direct* (1981), a French film in English, directed on Scottish locations by Bertrand Tavernier, with a screenplay by him and David Rayfiel based on David Compton's novel *The Continuous Katherine Mortenhoe*. Katherine (Romy Schneider) works for a publishing company whose novels are written by computer; she is dying. Since death has become rare a television company wants to make a programme about it, and she agrees to be its subject, because her separated husband needs the money. Having got it, she disappears till befriended by Roddy (Harvey Keitel): she doesn't know that he works for the television company and that he has a camera inside his head. So, as they flee through the countryside, she does not know that the world is watching her, and he doesn't intend that she should know, especially after falling in love with her. The situation is very strong, and the last part of the film works partly through the views of Scotland and the introduction of Max Von Sydow – as Katherine's first husband – even if he is required to be the fount of all wisdom. Glaswegians may be alarmed to find some of the grimier parts of their city representing the city of the future.

A Swiss director, Alain Tanner, used Dublin and Eire for his view of a future society, in *Light Years Away/Les Années Lumières* (1981), based on *La Voie Sauvage* by Daniel Odier. A young barman and layabout, Jonas (Mick Ford), meets an elderly eccentric, Yoshka (Trevor Howard), whom he pursues to the junkyard where he does his experiments. He tries to bring order into the chaos, but in view of the man's hostility attempts to commit suicide by perishing in a fire of wrecked cars; the old man rescues him and nurses him back to health, during which time Jonas learns that he is manufacturing a pair of wings so that he can fly. Jonas is sent to catch an eagle, the only bird not sacrificed when Yoshka covers his body with bird blood. This is a simple fable and visually impressive, if overlong. You may be glad to find that there has not been a nuclear war by 2000 AD. Many films featuring wrecks in strange country-

sides turn out to be tales of carrying on after the final bang. They tend to be whoosy and, fortunately, not really of the genre.

One film of tangential interest should detain us briefly, if only because we glanced at its original: and Werner Herzog's *Nosferatu: Phantom der Nacht* (1979) acknowledges both Murnau's film and Bram Stoker's *Dracula* as its sources. Herzog makes hallucinating use of the waterfalls and boulders of Gothic revival landscapes, but has otherwise attempted a literal remake of the earlier film. Its best moment comes at the end, when Lucy Harker (Isabelle Adjani) clutches Count Dracula (Klaus Kinski), sacrificing herself, for she knows that vampires can be vanquished if they linger beyond cockcrow – and she seems to be in sexual ecstasy. And the final shots of Harker (Bruno Ganz), red-eyed and fanged, the evil replacement for the dead Count, are also haunting.

If we stay in the past it is because John Boorman's *Excalibur* (1981) is as successful as his *Zardoz* was not. He wrote the screenplay from *Le Morte Darthur* with Rospo Pallenberg, and they have availed themselves of the cinema's capacity for magic. Their text is not entirely clear and nor, indeed, their images, since they have conceived the Dark Ages as dark, which rather makes nonsense of Camelot, which has no shining hour: things are glum even at its peak. At times the images are breathtaking, if in the manner of Spielberg and Lucas; while elsewhere it is apparent that the PreRaphaelites provided inspiration. If there is one thing in common between the Brotherhood and the so-called movie brats it is a wish to stun with their own virtuosity, but while both have a certain panache they are essentially second-rate, superficial and visually dexterous but not nearly as clever as they think they are. Boorman too often shows his dependence: the

About once in every decade, it seems, the Arthurian legends get a going-over by the movies. In 1954 there was The Knights of the Round Table *and in 1967 the musical,* Camelot. *John Boorman's 1981 version was called* Excalibur *– which qualifies as a genre film because it takes several opportunities to show magic performed.*
Opposite: *Nicol Williamson as Merlin.*
Right: *Nigel Terry and Cherie Lunghi as Arthur and Guinevere and, behind them, Liam Neeson as Gawaine.*

Some of Ray Harryhausen's creations from his most ambitious and successful venture, Clash of the Titans. **Right:** *Perseus (Harry Hamlin) and his first encounter with the winged horse, Pegasus.* **Below:** *Andromeda (Judi Bowker) at the mercy of Thetis's monstrous son, Calibos (Neil McCarthy).* **Opposite, top:** *The temple of Medusa, with that formidable she-monster preparing to defend her lair.*

music, for instance, borrows freely from Wagner, but at one point moves into a chant similar to one in *Camelot*, Lerner and Loewe's musical on the same theme. His movie shows greater understanding of the legends and feuds of the Dark Ages than did Lerner in his screenplay for the film version of *Camelot*, but as the ladies line up for the joust they recall the Ascot guests in a more famous Lerner-Loewe musical. The mask worn by Mordred recalls *Zardoz*; *Seven Samurai* is not too far away; while the performances often resemble those in the several films debunking or revising the myths of the old American West. Nicol Williamson is made to play Merlin as a comic looney; this actor always did have trouble making his vowel sounds sound like those of other people, and Boorman has had him emphasize their strangeness, with the result that this Merlin is strange-peculiar instead of strange-haunting. On one hand Boorman wants this to be a Camelot for the '80s, bloody, anti-war, full of the vileness and foolishness of men, but on the other he refuses to let go the splendid, heroic ideas and the possibility of visual splendour which they present. The contests of magic and the transformation scenes are memorable additions to those done in the genre.

The same is true of the tricks and special effects in *Clash of the Titans* (1981), Ray Harryhausen's masterpiece. It is obvious which of the strange creatures are models, for they move jerkily. The Gorgon's head is not as frightening as it might be; a mechanical golden owl – ordered by Zeus (Laurence Olivier) to be a guide to Perseus (Harry Hamlin) is too much like R2-D2 in *Star Wars* for its own good. Yet the special effects are often thrilling. Every other frame communicates Harryhausen's love of movies and of the Greek Myths – a love shared by the director, Desmond Davis, and by the writer, Beverly Cross, though he has provided some flat dialogue and some twists not found in the usual sources. Olympus, however, is the conventional place of columns and swirling mists. Zeus discloses himself as protective towards Perseus, thus irritating Thetis (Maggie Smith), for her own son, Calibos (Neil McCarthy) has turned into a misshapen beast. The two men are destined to be mortal enemies, as Perseus struggles – eventually – to save his beloved, Andromeda (Judi Bowker) from the sea monster, the dreaded Kraken. He has the flying horse, Pegasus, to help him but apart from the Medusa – whose blood sprouts giant scorpions – Perseus is beset at every turn by the incredible creatures thought up by the Ancient Greeks – and splendidly visualized by Harryhausen. His producer, as is customary, is Charles H. Schneer, but this film was presented by MGM and not Columbia, which had distributed most of their others. It cost $15 million and was conceived in 1976, filmed in 1979, with a further two years for Harryhausen to work on the effects.

Its popularity was enormous, but not of the measure of *E.T.; the Extra-Terrestrial* (1982), which enchanted a generation of children while leaving some grown-ups disgruntled, including myself. It was a further triumph for Steven Spielberg, who saw its takings surpass every other film in history, including the *Star Wars* trio, at which point we should note in sixth place *Jaws*, which Spielberg

directed, and in the seventh *Raiders of the Lost Ark*, which he also directed and which George Lucas produced. Success of this order cannot be quarrelled with, though I've already said that it is a shame that their films do not have more humour – or, come to that, ingenuity. Spectacle they have enough; and hype. The publicity line on *The E.T.* was that Universal backed it without enthusiasm, and only because they had passed on *Star Wars*,

Little E.T. lost. The forlorn little alien who got left behind when the starship returned home.

Opposite: *The starship E.T. missed, soaring into the empyrean.*
Left: *But there's a friend for everyone in an ideal world, and E.T. finds one in Elliott (Henry Thomas).*
Below: *The escape. E.T. brings his own powers to play to help the children who are helping him return to the starship.*

Three astronauts (Veronica Cartwright, John Hurt and Tom Skerrit) answering a distress signal from a distant planet in Alien.

but it was being trailered in cinemas across the country four months before its New York premiere, instead of the usual two to three weeks. Full page ads began appearing in the trade press a month later, and then in the newspapers, so by the time the film opened – as with *Jaws, Raiders* and its 1984 sequel, *Indiana Jones and the Temple of Doom* – there was barely a literate adult or child who was not aware of its existence. However, all the publicity in the world cannot attract audiences if they are not interested, and unquestionably some spectators returned to *The E.T.* time and again. The audience with which I saw it was rapt, and presumably it was not, like vast sections of the media, impressed with success for its own sake. My own view is that its only element above the elementary is the chase, but the best of that had already been seen in *The Great Escape* (the bump-bump of the cycles over the ridges) and *Miracolo in Milano* (the taking to the air to escape the enemy). Also, I do not believe that small boys make friends with squidgey monsters, and the popularity of toy E.T.s would not make me believe otherwise. Teddy bears are not much like bears.

A small boy, Elliott (Henry Thomas) finds the alien in the woodshed and introduces him to his brother and sister, as guardsman search the area, suspecting that a departing spaceship has left behind one of its occupants. Elliott is fascinated with the E.T., who can stop flowers from wilting, can juggle balls in the air, can heal with his finger. He loves E.T., and why not, since the clever little creature is struggling to learn English? But nevertheless Elliott decides that he should go home and so leaves E.T. amidst a pile of gadgetry on a hill.

Inexorably drawn back to the hill, he finds that E.T. has been savaged by a dog. The creature is taken home to be cured, and in due course the 'enemy' arrives – doctors and scientists, all of whom (unlike the children) don masks to examine E.T. E.T. dies, but rallies, doubtless because of his telepathic communication with Elliott, who with his teenage brother (who had never driven before) spirits him away.

At one point the mother is discovered reading *Peter Pan* – that bit about 'Do you believe in fairies?' while the other schoolchildren tease Elliott about his 'gnome'. That may be disarming, but it is not innocent, for this movie is about as innocent as the World Trade Center in New York. Many people claimed that they loved the affection in the film, the trust between the child and the creature – but that was done so much better in some not-very-good films of Hollywood's golden age, such as *Lassie Come Home*. The laughter in the house (when I saw the film) was solely that of children. Presumably the adult admirers of this movie liked this portrait of the world turned upside down, where the goodies are the baddies. At its centre are two innocents, threatened and hounded by scientists and the very forces which should be protecting us. In a world seemingly bent on nuclear destruction it must be good to know that as in *Close Encounters of the Third Kind* man is bent on self-destruction while the aliens love children.

The E.T. itself was designed by Carlo Rambaldi, who had designed the aliens in *Close Encounter*; he also invented the special effects which play the title-role in *Alien* (1979), directed by Ridley Scott

Above: *John Hurt descends into the deepest recesses of an alien space ship, advancing towards the moment when a 'thing' will attach itself to him and make the homeward journey a nightmare for the crew of the* Nostromo.

Right: *Sigourney Weaver as Ripley, one of the crew, preparing for the final encounter.*

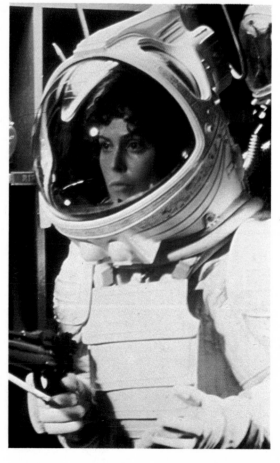

from a screenplay by Dan O'Bannon. Seven astronauts are returning to earth in their cavernous star ship, carrying 20,000,000 tons of mineral ore. They are roused from their long-term suspended animation to answer a distress call from an alien vessel on a nearby planet. Three of the crew visit the planet and find the vessel abandoned. One of them, Kane (John Hurt) becomes curious about some pod-like life forms and goes to examine one. The pod bursts open, ejecting an organism which wraps itself around his space helmet. The others carry the blinded Kane back to the ship where Ripley (Sigourney Weaver) refuses to admit them with the organism – which could prove dangerous to everyone on board. But the Science Officer, Ash (Ian Holm) goes against the quarantine regulations and opens the ports. Kane's helmet has been penetrated and the thing is locked tight over his face. But on the following day it detaches itself, which baffles the crew; it then falls, apparently dead, from the ceiling. Ash insists they must take it back to earth for investigation and Ripley, who took him to task for allowing it on board, grows increasingly suspicious of him. Kane, meanwhile, recovers and seems none the worse. The star ship is back on course and the crew will return to long-term sleep. They sit down for a meal – and suddenly Kane is a victim of violent pain. In a hair-curling sequence the Alien is born, erupting out of Kane's body and disappearing into the labyrinth of tunnels and corridors of the huge star ship. 'Don't touch it! Don't touch it!' yells Ash. No one wants to – but the Alien is loose and they are ten months from home. The captain (Tom Skerrit) seeks the advice of Ash, who as a proper man of science is as fascinated by the thing as any of his profession in film since the days of Méliès. The hunt is up, and the captain is the second victim, leaving Ripley in command and with access to the control-computer (Mother). What she discovers sets the scene for the confrontation with the dubious Ash – a scene which is a high-powered shocker. It becomes clear that the authorities' first interest is the Alien itself, not the lives of the crew, which places this film among those with a Dystopian view of the future. The crew fall victim one by one, until the sole survivor, Ripley, destroys the star ship and prepares for the final duel in the space module.

You may be reminded, if you have seen it, of *It! The Terror from Outer Space* a minor genre film of 1958 probably inspired by *Voyage of the Space Beagle*, by A. E. van Vogt. *It!* paralleled the action of its exact contemporary, *The Thing*, except that the threatened group of experts happened to be in flight and not in camp.

This was the situation, in a different form, of *Dr Cyclops*; it was also the basic situation of the genre, inasmuch as the most brilliant minds cannot cope with the uncontrollable. To that extent, *Alien* is satisfying; and the special effects, like the cast, are superior to most movies. But, as the critic John Simon wrote, the film 'has the usual number of inconsistencies, improbabilities, and outright absurdities characteristics of the sci-fi and horror genres'; and he concludes, because of its excessive bloodiness 'For fanciers of horror, among whose numbers I do not count myself, *Alien* is recommendable, provided that they are

free from hypocrisy and finicky stomachs'. *Alien* strives, successfully, to terrorize its audience. It is not speculating on the perils of the unknown – which may be said to be inflicted on those best able to cope with them, the men of space.

Society as a whole is threatened in *Blade Runner* (1982), also directed by Ridley Scott. In 2019 AD there is a breed of replicants – robots in human form, developed to do slave labour in space. Since there is the possibility of their developing emotions they are programmed to self-destruct after four years. However, they have a tendency to become unruly, and some members of the police force – blade runners – are detailed to kill on sight. Six Nexus 6 replicants have hijacked a shuttle and returned to earth, their purpose unknown, but it is probable that they wish to coerce the Tyrell Corporation, which manufactured them, to prolong their lives. The corporation's executives are programmed to discover which are people and which are replicants, and one is on the verge of discovery when the interviewee catapults him into the next world. A retired blade runner, Rick Deckard (Harrison Ford) is persuaded to track down the replicants, but the only evidence offered is a sheath of photographs and a clue in the form of a reptile's scale. Rick studies the photographs in private eye fashion, and makes the right deductions; but he cannot be sure whether any of his helpers are replicants, leading him on before killing him. He is involved in a number of death-defying battles which are tremendously exciting and if they, like the plot, do not really convince except in terms of

Two of those likely to be encountered by Harrison Ford in his work as a Blade Runner. One encounter (above) appears to have been successful; another (left) might have a different result. Under the make-up is Darryl Hannah.

What the streets of Los Angeles will look like in the next century. A glimpse of the impressive production design for Blade Runner.

myth that is neither here nor there. Half the time there is no valid reason for any of the characters being where they are; and if Ford has a 'Dragnet' type commentary that only emphasizes the various styles, plots and genres plagiarized. The film is all effect and no narrative, like the many close-ups of rivulets of rain. And what are we to make of the hints of bisexuality – as opposed to asexuality – in the male and female replicants?

The film's makers were surely meaning to create myths. Their source is a tale by Philip K. Dick, *Do Androids Dream of Electric Sheep?* which deserved better treatment. Hampton Fancher and David Peoples wrote the screenplay, while Douglas Trumbull's name heads those responsible for special photographic effects, and these are stunning. At ground level this Los Angeles is a fantasy of Chinatown, where much of the language is gibberish and garbage piles are high in the streets. The people are rude, oriental, indifferent, wandering listlessly, perhaps drugged, looking for some outre entertainments. It rains all the time. Above the city, seemingly designed after a study of the paintings of Max Ernst, are huge ads for another planet – 'Visit Offland' – and the face of a Chinese girl, also in lights. Small craft whizz to and fro, as they have since *Just Imagine* and *Things to Come* – or Spielberg's *1941*. Certainly Ford's hero is like the Indiana Jones he played for Spielberg – intrepid, stoic – and masochistic. When allowed a Bogart-like parody he suggests that there may be a real actor within the ikon. He has to be superhuman, because that is what his enemies are. And he has a superhuman will to survive.

So has the hero of *Outland* (1981), powerfully played by Sean Connery. It is the role that Gary Cooper played in *High Noon*, but the writer-director Peter Hyams has not followed the earlier film so slavishly as to be predictable. Where that had a very definite view of the old West this one feels equally strongly about the future – or that is, the future as encapsulated in a space station. It serves as a mining base, on Io, third moon of Jupiter, and like the small town in *High Noon* it is isolated from the main stream of civilization. It is too lonely for the new marshall's wife, so she has already returned home. He is O'Niel (Connery), required to keep order in a society where all human values are subordinate to the demand for high production. The other men do little in their leisure time but booze or lie on their beds; we see them at their ablutions but never reading a book or deep in discussion. Under the influence of drink and drugs they are violent towards each other or the women in the colony of hookers. One man locks himself up with one whom he threatens to murder after injecting – or inhaling ? – amphetamines.

As in *Alien*, the mood is horrific from the start. O'Niel discovers that the drugs are being supplied by the manager, Sheppard (Peter Boyle), regardless of the fact that at any time after sampling them the men become psychopathic. O'Niel's computer reveals that his deputy has been bribed by Sheppard, and that he has drug-pushers on his staff. Sheppard admits to distributing the drugs, if not with the management's approval or knowledge certainly to its advantage, for the men increase their output after spending their free time in a state of euphoria. O'Niel refuses to be bribed and learns from his computer that Sheppard has hired two killers from the base station, for Sheppard's job will be on the line if O'Niel isn't licked. 'I could use a little help,' says O'Niel in the canteen to his colleagues, indifferent to his danger. His new (black) deputy refuses to help, leaving as his sole ally a middle-aged woman doctor (Frances Sternhagen).

Hyams's view of the future is as chilling as any in cinema or literature, partly because of the importance that drugs and violence have achieved in our society. Surprisingly, in my view, this film was not received with general enthusiasm. It is a *High Noon* for the '80s, as the critic Clive Hirschhorn observed, noting that in 1954 the American poet and critic Horace Gregory had predicted that the Western movie was approaching its last round-up. 'Within another decade' Gregory had written, 'the noise of jet-propelled space rockets on TV sets will drown out, tune out the explosions sounding from the guns of the roaring West.'

As we have seen, it took longer than a decade. In general I have ignored the junky, Z-budget movies which retarded the progress of science-fiction in the cinema. The obvious home for fantasy was the Disney Organization, which indeed continued to interest itself in science-fiction after the success of *20,000 Leagues Under the Sea*. The greatest financial success in Disney's history concerned a flying governess, *Mary Poppins* (1964), and it was on that level, rather than the Jules Verne film, that the studio worked, making 'fun' films for all the family, such as *The Absent-Minded Professor* (1961), about a college professor who becomes the target for some crooks after inventing an anti-gravity substance. That was popular enough to merit a sequel, *Son of Flubber*, as was *The Misadventures of Merlin Jones* (1963), about another scientific genius who invents a machine that can read people's thoughts. Such later films as *The Computer Wore Tennis Shoes* (1970) and *The Cat From Outer Space* (1978) were much less well received and indeed by the time the latter was released Disney's hold on world audiences had considerably slackened. The several costly failures were offset by the reissues of the magnificent early cartoons and profits from the two theme-parks in California and Florida. Consequently the success of *Star Wars* stirred the Disney Organization as nothing since the death of Walt himself, for here was a children's fantasy achieving world approval while its own films were flopping. Not only had Disney lost its pre-eminence in that particular field, but it had done so while having on the staff writers, animators and technicians who were the world's acknowledged experts in dreaming up fantasies for the world's young moviegoers.

The answer was *The Black Hole* (1979), into which was poured all the Disney expertise and $20 million. A space-ship is returning to earth with its crew and the cutest little robot this side of *Star Wars*. The personnel discuss the danger of the Black Hole and one Dr Reinhardt who disappeared about there twenty years ago, while trying to discover habitable life in outer space. It is established that the lost space ship has the magnetism of the earth, and within seconds our crew are

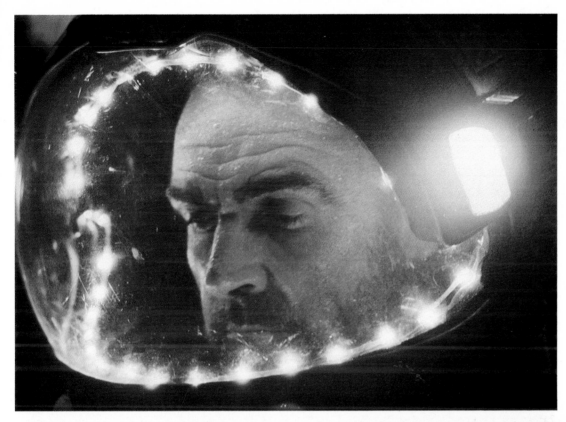

Left: *Sean Connery in* Outland. *In a performance of great authority he elicits considerable sympathy for the character's dilemma and contributes much to the film's effectiveness. He is the marshal on Io, one of Jupiter's satellites, and not a pleasant place to be, from where valuable minerals go back to earth.*

Below: *The workers preparing to descend to the mines of Io in* Outland.

Robot sentries in The
Black Hole *fight – and are
fought with – laser guns.*

Disney's Tron, *alas, comes
to life only fitfully – and
those occasions have much
to do with David Warner,
who plays the evil
Controller of the computer
games in which the hero
becomes embroiled.*

© Walt Disney Productions 1984

© Walt Disney Productions 1984

having trouble with theirs. Soon they are buckled on to the missing craft, on which they discover Dr Reinhardt (Maximilian Schell), looking more like Disney's Captain Nemo than is decent. He has created a series of robots, including Maximilian, whose only expression is an orange light and whose 'hands' can turn into buzz-saws – though why they should want to is a mystery except to the people who concocted this movie. As directed by Gary Nelson, it is often visually impressive, but apart from its raid on Verne it borrows only clichés – the stranded travellers, a seemingly benign but mad professor and danger at every corner. Even Anthony Perkins's astronaut captain turns out to be like the obsessed, half-balanced neurotics which this actor has played so often. And even children must reject the logistics – that one spacecraft can attach itself to another without programming, that the astronauts can move freely from one to the other, that the new one should be a chamber of horrors.

The film was a failure with the press and as its domestic takings were only $5 million above its cost it was not regarded by the industry as successful. Disney had similarly great expectations of *The Watcher in the Woods* (1980), directed in Britain by John Hough, and concerning an American girl (Lynn Holly Johnson) who is 'taken over' by the long-disappeared daughter of the old crone (Bette Davis) who owns the house in which the girl's family is living. The genre here is 'old dark house' and not science-fiction, as it is described on its Videocassette cover – but by the time that was issued the Disney Organization had become besotted with science-fiction. In this case the film was withdrawn after disastrous notices and business during its first week's run. The 'open' ending was reshot in Hollywood, by an uncredited Vincent McEveety, and when the film again emerged it was copyrighted as a 1982 American production. The ending was now fantastic – and not disappointing in the circumstances, which are not very elevated.

In the meantime, the Disney Organisation had a rethink about its purpose. Family audiences were long gone, though parents could be prevailed upon to take children to Disney movies in the school holidays. The bulk of audiences were comprised of teenagers and young adults, and it was for them that *Tron* (1982) was designed – largely by computer, though the credits for special effects were among the most lengthy ever issued. *Tron* is all special effects and no movie, being a jumble of abstracts tied to a thin plot in which a computer expert is programmed into a Video game influenced, one imagines, by the one in *Rollerball*. A further inspiration seems to have been the psychedelic trip in *2001*. It was widely reported that some moviegoers smoked marijuana to turn on during that sequence, and it was also said of *Fantasia* when Disney reissued that in the '60s. Disney executives cannot be blamed for it, but I do not think, in their relentless pursuit of profits, that it bothered them. There were none from *Tron*, which cost $21 million and took just over $15 million in the domestic market. The director, Steven Lisberger, who wrote the screenplay from a story he co-authored, had only one major (if that) credit, *Animalympics*. Unlike *The Black Hole*, which was made by committee, *Tron* could be said to be the vision of one man; but it was a further grave error.

So, alas, was *Something Wicked This Way Comes* (1983), which had a budget of £23 million and was written off with a loss of $21 million. In this case Disney engaged a director with a first-class reput-

In Something Wicked This Way Comes *Mr Dark (Jonathan Pryce) has magic powers – or, alternatively, supporters with similar gifts such as the Dust Witch (Pam Grier), who hopes to silence the children (Vidal Peterson, Shawn Carson).*

What you may see if you venture into Mr Dark's carnival in Something Wicked This Way Comes – *and what you may encounter (**below**) if someone has ventured to ride on the time carousel.*

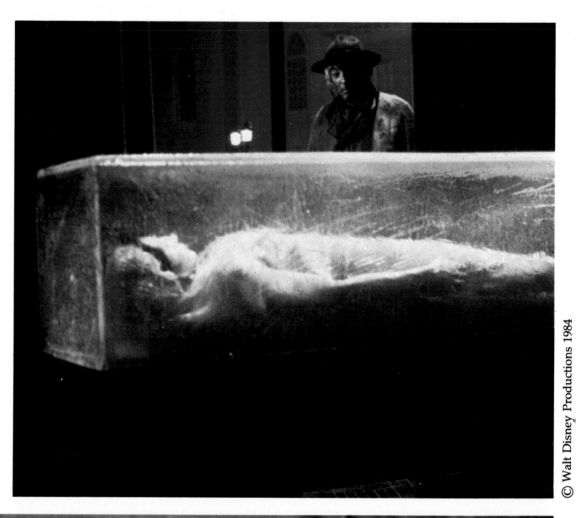

ation, Jack Clayton, and Ray Bradbury scripted from his own much-admired book. We have looked at some unsatisfactory films of Bradbury's work, and should commiserate with him on his poor luck with the film industry. In 1953 his screen treatment *The Meteor* became *It Came From Outer Space*, with little of his original work eventually included. In 1961 MGM commissioned him to write a screenplay based on his book of short stories, *The Martian Chronicles* but the film was never made. In 1974 Sam Peckinpah was to have directed Kirk Douglas in *Something Wicked This Way Comes* for 20th Century-Fox, but that too was cancelled. The Disney film seems to me a triumph, if flawed, and I can only suppose that *The Black Hole* and *Tron* had driven away the hitherto faithful Disney audience. The setting is a small Illinois town (though the locations were done in Vermont) in the '30s, in Autumn. The two boy heroes, Will (Vidal Peterson) and Jim Nightshade (Shawn Carson), are astonished to find the carnival arrive and are privy to the strange activities of its proprietor, Mr Dark (Jonathan Pryce). He is well-named, for he is in the fearsome business of granting the most secret wishes of his clients. He also uses both natural cunning and sorcery in attempts to scare the two boys to death. Will's father, Charles Halloway (Jason Robards), is powerless to help. Should either he or Jim fall into temptation, as seems probable, Will would be isolated – and the way the film conveys the classic situation of one terrorized small child against an evil world is just one reason why this is a superior entertainment.

It is Clayton's best film since *The Innocents*, based on a not dissimilar tale of the supernatural, Henry James's *The Turn of the Screw*. His biggest mistake was the miscasting of Mr Pryce, unkempt of hair and beard, eyes gleaming, a smile lurking, in the manner of Alan Badel in a celebrated short film, *The Stranger Left No Card*. What was needed was someone more suavely menacing, more powerful and even well-groomed, since it is implied that Dark belongs to the 1890s. There are faults of over-emphasis in both direction and script, particularly in Halloway's explanations to his son, but Bradbury's imaginative use of his sources, which include *Faust* and less obviously *Dracula*, is impressive. We are not far from the world of vampires and when Dark wills on Halloway the experience of death the expression on Robards' face is that we associate with sexual ecstasy. The dearest wishes are sexual, or so we may assume. They are sinister in this context, but Halloway's temptation is cruel, for he wants to return to youth, which would deny him his son, while he wants to be youthful for the boy. If the other boy, Jim, jumps on the time carousel that could lead him into incest. At the same time, as I've said, this is a children's adventure, virtually of the eerie level of *The Night of the Hunter*, and much better made. The film's failure is sad, for it is both visually and intellectually satisfying, while relying on technological tricks for only a minimum. Others will undoubtedly attempt a rehabilitation.

None of us can yet say which will be the most enduring of the cinema's current outburst of fantasy, but I should be surprised if *Krull* (1983) were not one of them. In *The New York Times*, Janet Maslin gave what I think is the correct verdict – that it is 'a gentle, pensive sci-fi adventure film

Ken Marshall in Krull, fighting one of the androids which are the slaves of the evil creature which has brought such misery to the planet of Krull.

Terrifying and powerful,
the hero's chief adversaries
in Krull.

Terrifying and powerful,
the hero's chief adversaries
in Krull.

166

One of the slave androids self-destructs after being wounded in Krull.

that winds up a little too moody and melancholy for the *Star Wars* set, though that must be the audience at which it is aimed. . . And the mostly British cast performs with more delicacy than the usual gee-whiz adventure film requires. However, *Krull* is muted and unemphatic too. And for all its unusual touches it doesn't feel like anything new'. Indeed, no. This is a sword and sorcery epic set far in the future, with a villain whose followers are androids wielding ray-guns – and the heart may sink at that. The plot itself is similar to those of the Harryhausen films, and in particular *Sinbad and the Eye of the Tiger*, taking as it does the young hero and his companions on an odyssey. Both journeys are a quest; in the earlier film for a cure for a curse, in the later one to rescue a beautiful princess.

Both movies feature witchcraft and transformations, a learned sage with the secret needed by the hero, a giant creature (a troglodyte, a cyclops) who turns out to be friendly, and a climactic battle in a building on the verge of collapsing (or self-destructing). However, the magical effects in *Krull* show advances miraculous when set beside Harryhausen's pioneering work. Director Peter Yates and writer Stanford Sherman and their team have taken extra care to make the effects seamless, to render as if newly minted the now-familiar ingredients borrowed equally from legend and old sci-fi movies. By logical standards that climactic battle is absurd: the villain is so powerful, his fortress so impregnable, his warriors so invincible that our

heroes are unlikely opponents, even with their fortitude, foolhardiness and own (selective) magical powers. This does not matter; the film's defects no longer matter, nor the inadequacy of the two leading players (Ken Marshall, Lysette Anthony) for the film has – with skill, imagination and technical expertise – made everyone of us a child again, lost in wonder because David has slain Goliath, Jack has become the giant-killer. Fantasy has once again confirmed our earliest convictions.

This survey has been written out of the upsurge of interest in science-fiction in the last few years. I have been able to see, or see again, every film I have discussed, and was soon bewildered by the variety, which is not restricted to Dystopian predictions and men in space-suits being faced with apparently insuperable problems. As I write there are so many genre films in production – parodies, comedies, mysteries, adventures – that the public may turn away as it has turned against Westerns. There should be something in most of them to be savoured, however, when people look back as I have done in this book. Undoubtedly my greatest pleasure has been the imaginative powers utilized in putting the future, the unknown, on the screen, though I have loved, too, the special effects that allow Superman to fly over Manhattan or any spacecraft to take off for Mars. It is sad that it took so long for the film industry to realize what Méliès knew, that fantasy and cinema should be inseparable partners.

ACKNOWLEDGMENTS

Photographs The Publishers would like to thank Michelle Snapes and her staff at The National Film Archive, and all the staff at The Kobal Collection for their invaluable assistance during the compilation of this book.

Colour Hamlyn Picture Library 88–89; The Kobal Collection, London endpapers, title page, 38, 39, 43 bottom, 50–51, 55, 58–59, 62–63, 66, 69 bottom, 73, 74–75, 76, 78, 79 top, 79 bottom, 81 top, 92, 98 top, 101, 102 top, 102–103, 104, 105 top, 105 bottom, 106–107, 108–109, 109 bottom, 120, 122 bottom, 126–127, 135 top, 135 bottom, 136–137, 138, 139 top, 139 bottom, 140–141, 143, 145 top, 145 bottom, 146 top, 146 bottom, 147, 148, 149, 150 top, 150 bottom, 151 top, 151 bottom, 152, 153 top, 153 bottom, 156 top, 157 top, 157 bottom, 158–159, 161 top, 161 bottom, 162 top, 165, 166–167, 168; The National Film Archive, London 14–15, 72, 77 top, 77 bottom, 84, 87, 91, 93 bottom, 94, 95, 96, 98 bottom, 99, 110–111, 112 top, 112 bottom, 116 top, 116 bottom, 117, 119 top. 119 bottom, 121, 122 top, 123, 125 top, 125 bottom, 128, 129, 130, 131, 132–133, 144, 154–155, 156 bottom; David Shipman 22; Walt Disney Productions 162 bottom, 164 top, 164 bottom.

Black and White Hamlyn Picture Library half title page, 19 right, 20; The Kobal Collection, London 24–25, 37 bottom, 40 top, 43 top, 45, 46, 49 top, 48–49, 53 bottom, 56, 61, 86 bottom, 90 top, 90 bottom, 93 top, 100, 113, 114, 115, 124, 163; The National Film Archive, London contents, 10–11, 13 top, 13 bottom, 16 top, 16 bottom, 18, 19 left, 21 top, 21 bottom, 23, 24 top, 24 bottom, 26, 27, 28, 29, 30, 31, 32–33, 33, 34–35, 37 top, 40 bottom, 41, 44, 47 top, 47 bottom, 52, 53 top, 54, 57, 60 top, 60 bottom, 64, 67, 69 top, 70, 71, 81 bottom, 82 top, 82 bottom, 83, 86 top.

Many of the illustrations in this book come from stills issued to publicise films made or distributed by the following companies or individuals:
UFA; London Films; Arthur Robinson; Prana; Decla-Bioscop; George Loureau; H. Geleen; Brigitte Helm; Gustav Ucicky; Rex Ingram; MGM; M. L'Herbier; Cinegraphic; First National; Mezhrabpom; Méliès; Universal; Famous Players-Lasky Corp.; Paramount; 20th Century-Fox; Lucasfilm; Gaumont; Republic; Fox; RKO; Hammer; Exclusive; Galaxy; George Pal; U-I; Winchester; Allied Artists; Walter Wanger; Columbia; Morningside; Walt Disney Productions; Anthony Nelson Keys; Associated General; Apjac; Philip Yordan; Chaumiane; Filmstudio; Marianne; Dino de Laurentiis; Stanley Kubrick; Devonshire; Greenlawn; National Periodical Publications; William Dozier; American Zoetrope; Frankovich-Sturges; Michel Gruskoff; Douglas Trumbull; SKM; Ameran; Robert Wise; John Boorman; Warner Brothers; United Artists; Norman Jewison; Polaris; British Lion; Paul N Lazarus III; EMI; Vanadas; The Ladd Co; Gamman; Alexander Salkind; Onion Pictures; Famous; Starling; Brandywine.

Every effort has been made to trace all present copyright holders of this material whether companies or individuals. Any unintentional omission is hereby apologised for in advance, and we should of course be pleased to correct any errors in acknowledgments in any future edition of this book.

Front Jacket: *The Image Bank.* J. Sohm.
Back Jacket: (inset top) *Outland.* The Kobal Collection.
(inset bottom) *Barbarella.* The National Film Archive, London.
(background) *The Ilustrated Man.* The National Film Archive, London.